Just-Right Writing Mini-Lessons Grade 1

by

Cheryl M. Sigmon and Sylvia M. Ford

NEW YORK · TORONTO · LONDON · AUCKLAND · SYDNEY
MEXICO CITY · NEW DELHI · HONG KONG · BUENOS AIRES

Dedications

To all teachers of beginning writers who support these young students through mini-lessons, ensuring that their students have a successful start on their writing journey.

And to Wendy Murray, our editor, who encouraged the "sparkle."
—SMF and CMS

To all the first-grade teachers who allowed me to observe and to teach their students. Once again, to my family for their support and encouragement.
—SMF

To my husband, Ray, for his constant love and support through my days of writing.
—CMS

Scholastic Inc. grants teachers permission to photocopy the reproducible pages in this book only for personal classroom use. No other part of this publication may be reproduced in whole or in part, or stored in a retrieval system, or transmitted in any form or by any means, electronic, mechanical, photocopying, recording, or otherwise, without written permission of the publisher. For information regarding permission, write to Permissions Department, Scholastic Inc., 557 Broadway, New York, NY 10012.

Cover design concept by James Sarfati
Interior design by LDL Designs
Cover photo by Paul Blair
Interior photos by Sylvia Ford

ISBN 0-439-43116-6
Copyright © 2004 by Cheryl M. Sigmon and Sylvia M. Ford
All rights reserved. Published by Scholastic Inc.
Printed in the U.S.A.
8 9 10   23 09 08 07 06

Table of Contents

Introduction

Mini-Lessons

Section Four: Making Writing Better (Revisions) 59

Mini-Lessons

Section Five: Writing for Real Purposes and Audiences 77

Mini-Lessons

Section Six: Publishing Our Writing
Mini-Lessons

Appendix

Bibliography

Please note: The order of the Table of Contents is not necessarily the order
in which the lessons will be taught throughout the year.

Acknowledgments

For writing samples, photos, and ideas:

B-C Grammar No. 1, Lexington School District Two, West Columbia, SC.
Teacher: Gloria Beatson

Center for Knowledge, Richland School District Two, Columbia, SC. Principal: JoLane Hall

Congaree/Wood Early Childhood Center, Lexington School District Two, West Columbia,
SC. Teachers: Cathy Roof and Becky Baker

Effingham Elementary School, Rincon, GA. Teacher: Marian Hodge

Monmouth Elementary School, North Adams Community Schools, Decatur, IN.
Teacher: Diana Arnold

North Adams Community Schools, Decatur, IN. Consultant: Rhonda Hays

Pineview Elementary School, Lexington School District Two, West Columbia, SC.
Teachers: Allison Lyles and Ms. Reid

Saluda River Academy for the Arts, Lexington School District Two, West Columbia, SC.
Teachers: Genie Williamson and Heather Woolery

Springdale Elementary School, Lexington School District Two, West Columbia, SC.
Teachers: Teresa Cartner and Wendy Keaton

For the opportunity to teach beginning writers the writing mini-lessons:

Kokomo City Schools, Kokomo, IN. Consultant: Kay Kinder

Lexington City Schools, Lexington, NE. Consultant: Julie Otero

6th District School, Covington Independent Schools, Covington, KY. Principal: Tony Ross

Monmouth Elementary, North Adams Community Schools, Decatur, IN
Teachers: Diana Arnold, Cheryl Hisner, Sheila August, and Marie Whitacre

New Franklin Elementary School, Portsmouth Schools, Portsmouth, NH.
First Grade Teachers and Cindy Matthews, Constance Carmody, and Diane Law

Northwest Elementary, North Adams Community Schools, Decatur, IN
Teachers: Jackie Morgan, Nancy Hodge, and S. Sailsbery

Southeast Elementary, North Adams Community Schools, Decatur, IN
Teachers: Sharon Rich, Cindy Engle

Introduction

How to Use This Book

Our intent in sharing these mini-lessons is to show how to integrate all that needs to be taught in the area of writing into a powerful instructional context: real writing! Many of us were not taught how to write well when we were in school. We were given writing assignments, but our teachers rarely instructed us about the attributes of quality writing. The thinking was that children first needed to learn proper mechanics, grammar, and usage to express their thoughts and ideas correctly. Writing assignments were often graded for correctness rather than for qualities of voice, use of figurative language, idea development, and other elements of composition. Those goodies were emphasized much later, in high school or college.

Gone are those days! We now realize that *assigning* writing isn't *teaching* it. Instruction must be direct and explicit to have an impact on students. And writing must happen in the context of something that makes sense to students: it must be for authentic purposes and real audiences. As for proper use of conventions, they have their place but they don't make writing better, only cleaner.

Modeling writing daily, where we show rather than tell students about the attributes of effective communication, leads students to those "ah-ha!" moments of understanding: "That's why I need a capital letter at the beginning of a sentence!" and "Oh, that's why I need a quotation mark where my character speaks!" or "That makes my writing so much clearer!" When we model daily all that we want students to learn about writing, the transfer to their own writing is more likely to occur. Writing becomes for them a familiar, purposeful activity.

And so you'll find this to be a book of the daily lessons you might model in short, powerful "sound bytes" of time in the framework of a Writing Workshop. The lessons usually fit into a 10-minute time period for the modeling portion of the workshop. After you model for the class, students will have a chance to write—hopefully having absorbed some of what you have shown them. Students are *not* expected to write about what you, the teacher, write about in your modeling. They're not even necessarily expected to practice the lesson's skill that very day. These skills will be reinforced in subsequent lessons as a constant reminder of what constitutes good writing, and of the options available to writers.

How the Mini-Lessons Were Selected

Good instruction in the classroom is usually based on two things: 1) the needs of the students as evidenced by their writing and their conversations; and 2) the curriculum provided by the school, district, or state that defines what students should know and be able to do at their grade level.

As the teacher, you determine the needs of your students and use this information to shape your instruction. If most of your students need more guidance with a particular aspect of writing, then an all-class mini-lesson is in order; if you see an isolated need, pull together a small group of students for a mini-lesson or deliver the instruction during an individual conference. We don't pretend to know your students well enough to suggest that there is a perfect match between the mini-lessons in this book and their precise needs. However, after many years of experience, we feel we can reassure you that, with some tweaking here and there, you'll be close!

Curriculum guides also inform teachers' decisions about mini-lessons. Most teachers feel that it would be foolish not to align instruction, curriculum, and district/state assessment. And it is hoped that this curriculum reflects the criteria that teachers feel represent elements of good, quality writing at their grade level.

In developing this book, we took the curriculum standards of 11 states, representing different geographic areas around the country. We then mapped these standards to find the most common writing objectives shared among these states. The mini-lessons spring from there; they show you how to incorporate those objectives/standards into the natural context of your teaching. We attempt to show students how the use of these standards really does help their writing become clearer and more powerful. We hope that the mini-lessons serve to motivate your students to write by showing them how easy it is and how much it affects others.

> The state standards used to develop curriculum for this book are: California, Colorado, Florida, Indiana, Missouri, New York, Pennsylvania, South Carolina, Texas, Virginia, Washington, and the National Standards (IRA/NCTE).

Sequencing Your Lessons

The lessons in this book do not necessarily appear in the order in which you should teach them throughout the year. They are, instead, organized by the purposes for which they are taught. With the exception of the first section, **Teaching Basic Concepts,** which should occur at the very beginning of the year, the other sections should be viewed as a menu. Pick and choose appropriately based on your students' needs and on opportunities to integrate lessons with other content you're teaching.

Consider these hints when designing the appropriate sequence of lessons in your classroom:

- Integrate some of the lessons from the **Planning for Writing** section with the **Teaching Basic Concepts** lesson so that the instruction is multi-leveled for those students who come to school with the basics and are ready to write organized pieces.

- Giving students too many ideas about planning for their writing might overwhelm them. Offer something new for their repertoire of planning strategies every few weeks. Especially in the beginning, don't let your students get stressed about formal planning at all. Convey that "writing is telling" and that it's as basic as talking—they should just do it! Use the lessons in the **Planning for Writing** section that pertain to gathering ideas.

- Mix lessons from Sections 3 to 6 throughout the year. Even simple, informal publishing can be done early in the year with little books (see page 100) and class books (see page 99). More formal publishing will be done later in the year, after writing is a little more "worthy" of individual publishing.

- Don't teach all of the Section 3 lessons on **Making Writing Clearer and Cleaner** in succession, as that may convey that writing has to be correct to be acceptable or good. Mix lessons on grammar, mechanics, and usage with the lessons on revision found in the **Making Writing Better** section.

- Sprinkle lessons from the **Writing for Real Purposes and Audiences** section throughout the year so that students will have a clear understanding that writing has real application to their everyday lives.

- When you're teaching interesting content in Science, Social Studies, or Health, or when you're reading something interesting in your Guided Reading, make connections to the lessons on informational pieces in the **Writing for Real Purposes and Audiences** section.

Take time to read through the Table of Contents and think about the other content you teach as you design the scope and sequence of lessons for the year.

The Mini-Lessons as Part of the Writing Workshop

The Writing Workshop is traditionally divided into three parts: 1) the teacher's model lesson; 2) the students' writing time; and 3) time for students to share what they've been working on. This book deals with the first segment, the model lesson. This segment is when the teacher writes for students daily. Modeling may be done in any number of ways, but

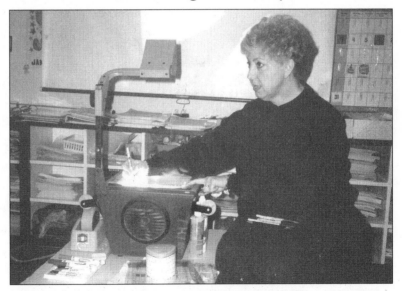

A first-grade teacher models writing for her students.

generally includes the teacher sitting down to compose at the overhead projector while students observe. You might instead prefer to stand beside chart paper. We favor sitting down at the overhead projector, as it models a natural writing posture for students. Because this modeling segment serves as direct, explicit instruction, it may not be as interactive as instruction during other parts of the day.

As you model, face the class to allow your students to watch and listen as you make the decisions that writers make when they compose. Your daily writing materials might include:

- Transparencies with lines similar to the lined paper students will use (see Appendix, page 108).
- An expandable folder or three-ring binder to store many of the writing samples you produce.
- Dividers for your folder or binder to catalog the types of writing and the skills you teach.
- Transparency pens in multiple colors.

If you don't have access to an overhead projector, model writing on chart paper or even on a chalkboard or dry-erase board (though these don't allow you to save your compositions). You'll still need pens or chalk in a variety of colors.

Your 10-minute model lesson for beginning writers will serve several primary purposes, all of which are important. It will:

- Model how writers get their ideas.
- Model the basic conventions of writing.
- Model good writing habits.
- Model the writing process.
- Offer writing options to students.
- Model the application of phonics to the printed page.
- Motivate students to write.

Thinking Aloud During the Mini-Lessons

Just as some students don't know how to engage their minds as they read, some don't know how to think about writing as they compose. Modeling the decisions that a writer must make, even the minor ones, allows those thought processes to become part of your students' habits. To that end, the lessons in this book all require that you, the teacher, not only model the actual writing but also the mental processes involved in composing. "Thinking aloud," as it's called, requires that you express aloud the decisions that writers must make as they write. For example, instead of just writing the word *whales* for the title of your piece, say, "We've been studying about whales for several weeks, and I think I could share a lot about what I've learned about them. I think I'll just write the word *whales* as my title. Titles are usually in the center at the very top of the paper, so let me write it there. Now, as I write, my title will remind me what I'm writing about so that I'll be sure to stick to the topic."

If you've never tried a "think aloud" with your students, it might seem a bit awkward at first. So many things have become automatic for us as mature writers that it's difficult to slow down and think deliberately about what we do and why we do it. After practicing the think aloud for several days or a few weeks, you'll soon find that it gets much easier.

Beyond These Lessons

Most schools have approximately 180 days of instruction. This book has 75 lessons. A little quick math tells us that you would need to create many of your own lessons if you were to use each of these once. However, we don't expect any teacher to teach the concepts and skills included in this book only one time. Even with the brightest classes, the lessons need to be retaught often. So instead of making up a lot of additional lessons, repeat the ones here that will most benefit your students.

Another reason for repeating lessons and not moving through skills and strategies too quickly is the phenomenon that some teachers describe as "the point of saturation." Around the midpoint of the year, students who have been like little sponges, absorbing everything possible, find that they've absorbed all that they can for the time being. They need sufficient time to practice what they've learned without encountering additional knowledge to process. So repeat what you model to reinforce lessons for your students.

Our hope is that this book will make it easier for you to plan your own lessons whenever you need to. For example, if we were teaching students about using simple quotations in their writing, one direct lesson would definitely not suffice! Students need repeated exposure to the intricacies of using dialogue. After teaching the lesson in this book, just repeat the same format and create a similar composition in which dialogue is the main focus.

Remember, too, that you'll need to consult with your own curriculum guide to be sure that you're addressing all of the standards and objectives dictated for your classroom. Put your curriculum guide side by side with the Table of Contents of this book and check off the standards the book addresses. Then make note of the ones that aren't addressed, and fill in the gaps so that no standard or objective is left without direct instruction to teach it.

We sincerely hope that these mini-lessons will help make Writing Workshop a fun time of day for you and your students!

Grade 1 Standards

Standard	1	2	3	4	5	6	7	8	9	10	11	12	13	14	15	16	17	18	19	20	21	22	23	24	25	26	27	28	29	30	31	32
Recognize print represents spoken language	√																															
Demonstrate print moves left to right/top to bottom		√																														
Print legibly, form letters, space			√							√	√																					
Use mixture of drawing and writing				√																												
Pre-write using graphic organizers/lists														√	√	√																
Focus on one topic												√	√	√	√	√										√						
Write brief personal narratives																															√	
Write using correct conventions																		√	√	√	√	√	√	√	√	√	√	√	√	√	√	√
Write in complete sentences																	√	√	√	√			√	√	√	√						
Capitalization: (first word in sentence, I, names)																				√	√	√				√						
Use end punctuation																							√	√	√	√						
Use correct spellings (freq. words/patterns)						√																				√						
Use classroom resources for spelling						√	√																									
Write using sequence (letters/sounds)					√	√																										
Publish variety of texts																																
Engage in sustained writing													√																			
Record questions for investigating																																
Write in response to what is read																																
Write for different purposes/audiences																																
Use writing process: pre-write												√	√	√	√	√	√															
Use writing process: draft							√	√	√																							
Use writing process: revise																																
Use writing process: edit																										√						√

33	34	35	36	37	38	39	40	41	42	43	44	45	46	47	48	49	50	51	52	53	54	55	56	57	58	59	60	61	62	63	64	65	66	67	68	69	70	71	72	73	74	75
																																				√							
					√								√																					√								
									√	√																																
√																																										
			√																													√										
	√						√																																			
								√	√	√																																
																		√	√	√	√				√	√			√							√	√	√	√	√	√	√
																√	√																									
																												√														
																											√		√				√									
		√			√			√	√	√	√			√	√			√	√	√	√	√	√	√	√	√	√			√	√	√	√	√		√	√	√	√	√	√	√
																																				√						
		√	√	√	√	√			√	√	√	√	√	√	√	√	√	√	√	√	√	√	√	√	√	√				√	√	√	√	√		√	√	√				
		√	√	√		√	√	√	√	√	√	√	√	√	√	√	√																			√						
	√																																			√				√		

Section One: Teaching Basic Concepts

Gauging What Students Are Ready For

For emergent language learners, writing is a critical part of figuring out what sounds, letters, and words are all about. For that very reason, in Balanced Literacy programs, writing is considered one of the major approaches to teaching children how to read. Lucy Calkins may have

A first grader thinks as she writes.

expressed it best when she said, "Writing is reading from the inside out." When children want to express themselves through written words, they first go through a process called *encoding*—matching letters and sounds in their minds in order to put something on paper. To decipher the print on the page, they must again match letters and sounds in their minds in a process referred to as *decoding*. So encoding and decoding could

Many beginning writers experiment with written language by stretching out the sounds they hear in words they want to use.

actually be thought of as reversed processes—making Calkins's quote precisely right! As proficient writers, adults often forget the effort that goes into these processes—the effort it takes, for example, for emergent writers to form each letter.

Much of writing in the early part of the school year is merely bringing children beyond an awareness level of encoding and decoding to the point of applying their phonetic understanding. They must have a great deal of practice at matching letters, sounds, and symbols before they build any fluency in expressing their ideas on paper. But even in the beginning of the year, we can give these students a chance to write daily.

Children take a while to work through the developmental stages of writing, and you must be patient during this time. Your role throughout much of this evolutionary process is to keep students motivated and to offer good models for their writing efforts. They need constant validation that their developmental stages, though they may not look like yours, are acceptable and acknowledged as "real" writing. **This first section, Teaching Basic Concepts, is intended to show you how to accomplish this validation.** Building confidence in students by convincing them that they are, indeed, writers greatly aids in fluency building.

First-grade teachers are more likely than teachers at other grade levels to see a wide range of writing stages among their students—even in the first week of school! Here are developmental stages you might witness in beginning writers:

Picture Writing. Some students only realize that writing can be represented through drawing objects they're talking about. They don't know how to use letters and words yet to express thoughts. Model this stage for students by saying, "Here's how some of you might be telling us things today," and then by drawing pictures to represent your ideas. (See lesson on page 23.)

"Driting." Driting is merely a combination of drawing and writing (Cunningham, et al, 1999). In this stage, students clearly make the connection between pictures that represent ideas and the symbols of letters that can be used to represent them. Model the transition from the picture stage to driting by drawing what you're telling about, then labeling the picture with words.

Scribble Writing. Some students write by making a series of loops or marks on their paper.

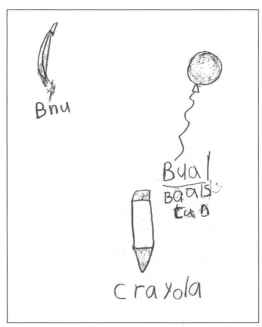

A child "drites" by connecting his drawings and letter symbols.

This is sometimes referred to as pretend writing but, for children, it's *real* writing! They are likely mimicking what they have observed adults doing. Introduce this stage by saying, "Here's what some of you might do as you're telling us things on your paper."

Random Letter Stage. In this stage of writing, sometimes called the pre-phonetic stage, students will attempt to write some of the letters they've noticed in their environment or that you have modeled for them. The letters are likely to be ill-formed because of underdeveloped fine motor skills, and they may be upside-down, backwards, and scattered about the page. These letters do not necessarily represent any particular words or sounds.

This student represented writing through drawing and experimenting with random letters.

Sounding Out Words. In this stage, the semi-phonetic stage, students begin to show that they are making attempts to apply their phonetic understanding. They usually represent beginning sounds as best they can and prominent phonemes (sounds) in the word based on what they understand the word to be. For example, a child might write *dress* as "jrs" or *make* simply as "mk," based on the sounds he hears as he pronounces the word. Students get tremendously excited in this stage because the teacher is often able to make out their words without any help!

"Sense of Sentence" Stage. This stage may still be semi-phonetic, but in it students show a clear understanding of how to form a complete thought on paper. Students may not always observe the correct conventions of punctuation in this stage, and their sentences are probably unsophisticated, but their ideas are clear.

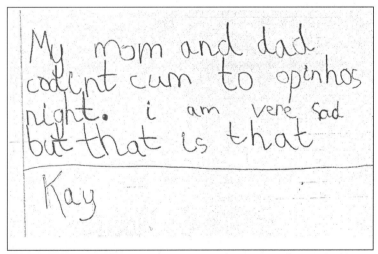

This student expressed complete thoughts, yet did not observe all of the basic conventions.

Pattern Writing Stage.
This is also referred to as the "love stage" of writing. Teachers of beginning writers are familiar with the type of writing that reads: "I love my mom. I love my dad. I love my sister. I love my bike." In this stage, students take comfort in familiar words and sometimes in copying words from around their environment.

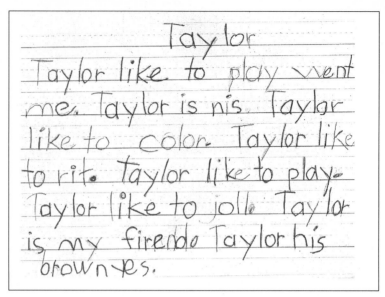

This student uses familiar words and sentence patterns.

"Sense of Story" Stage. The "story" here may not be a story in the sense of a narrative that has a beginning, middle, and end. However, in this stage, students create compositions that convey a feeling of completeness, with ideas that have some common thread. They might write three or more sentences about spring or about their dog—their ideas at last are cohesive! Students at this stage are in control of their writing. They begin to take risks with spelling big words phonetically in their rough-draft writing.

Conventional Writing. There are many stages of conventional writing—first-grade conventional writing doesn't look like that in third grade, which doesn't look like conventional writing in eighth grade. However, early conventional writing demonstrates that students can make a good attempt at applying their phonetic understanding, can link ideas together cohesively, and can apply many of the

This student demonstrates a sense of story by connecting several sentences to an idea or event.

conventions that make writing clear enough to read back with reasonable ease. This goal is attained with varying levels of success in the beginning; it's not achieved overnight. Early conventional writing requires a great deal of modeling and constant opportunities for practice.

In the beginning of the year, children will be everywhere on the continuum of developmental stages of writing. But all children, even those who write in a conventional way, have the potential for growth. Your mini-lessons at the start of the Writing Workshop each day will focus on what you've determined most or all of your

> This weekend I am going to my mountain house I am spending the nights. I can not wait. It wil be my second time. The last time I went was when Greer was a baby. She liked to crawl up and down the stairs Zackarey and Thomas aldan came with us. I do not rember my dad told me about the montain house After school when I will go home and pack.

This writer applied many basic conventions to cohesive ideas.

students need in order to help them mature in their writing. Remember that there will also be opportunities to help students grow individually during their daily writing time. You'll have ample time to give some students extra work with stretching out sounds to spell words, to help other students come up with ideas to write about, to teach still others about development of ideas, and even to nurture the occasional student who's writing "the great American novel"!

Start slowly with your mini-lessons and remember that teaching the basic concepts provides an important foundation for communicating effectively in the written language. You don't want students merely going through the motions that writing involves. In teaching mathematics, you wouldn't want students computing numbers without understanding the underlying concepts of why and how numbers work the way they do. Similarly, we don't want students scribbling or drawing without the knowledge of basic print and language concepts.

What we say, we can write

EXPLANATION: One of the earliest mini-lessons focuses on how print represents what we have to say. We write to communicate in the same way we talk to communicate.

SKILL FOCUS

Understand that print represents spoken language and conveys meaning

QUICK HINTS

Here are other opportunities to impress upon students that what we say, we can write:

- Refer to the Morning Message as a time that you want to talk to students in writing rather than by speaking.
- Use a whole-group End of the Day Journal as a time that students help you to tell in writing what has taken place during the day.
- Frequently model writing notes to yourself as you talk about things you need to remember in the class.
- Try writing notes on the board of important items that have been shared orally on the morning announcement.

STEPS

1. Tell students that you spoke over the telephone with someone. Explain to them that you can write in words what was said. For example, say:

   "My daughter Susan called me last night and asked me to send her a book that she needs for a class at Clemson University. This is what I told her."

   Or write:

   "Susan, the book that you asked for is on the bookshelf. It took me almost an hour to find it! When you come home, we will organize those books. I will wrap the book and send it in the mail to you."

2. Read the words to and with students. Explain to them that the words represent the phone conversation. Ask the students to share a time when their conversation was written down; for example, when they left someone a telephone message.

3. Share other examples of messages we write that convey what we might also say—*Happy birthday to you; Pick up Jake at soccer practice; Remember the pizza party on Friday!*

Direction of print

EXPLANATION: The print concept that we read and write words from the left of the page to the right is certainly basic. Introduce and reinforce this concept by guiding and tracking print with a finger or a pointer as you read text to students. Likewise, always make a point of starting your writing on the left and moving to the right.

SKILL FOCUS

Know that print moves left-to-right across the page and top-to-bottom

QUICK HINTS

After modeling this lesson several times, let students take turns holding the pointer to guide the class in a re-reading of the Morning Message.

Also, try reproducing one of the sentences from the Morning Message on a sentence strip. While students' watch, cut the words of the sentence strip apart. Let students help you reconstruct the sentence in a pocket chart. After trying this on several occasions, see if they can do it without your assistance.

STEPS

1. Write a simple Morning Message to students to greet them each day. Let them observe as you write to them. Start with just a couple of sentences in the first weeks of school and progress as students' understanding grows and their attention spans increase. Ask students to notice how you always write words and sentences starting on the left and moving to the right. Your example might look like this:

    August 10

    Dear Boys and Girls,
    Today our principal is coming to visit with us. We are
    excited that we will learn more about him!
    Love,
    Mrs. Wright

2. As you write, say the words out loud, pausing between each word so that children will be able to make a match between spoken and written language.

3. Use your finger or a pointer to read the message once or twice after you have completed it.

4. Invite students to help you read back the messages that you write, using the pointer as they read along with you. Have them read with you a couple of times so that those who can't read the real words will have an opportunity to repeat some of the words they remember from the first reading.

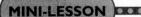

Recognizing the "quiet" spaces between words

EXPLANATION: The concept of words as separate units is a difficult one for children to grasp as they begin to make the transfer from spoken to written words. When we talk, we slur our words together. Rarely do we clearly enunciate every word, pausing between each. No wonder it's difficult to help children distinguish those separate units as they put words on paper!

SKILL FOCUS

Understand that written words are separated by spaces

QUICK HINTS

A glove stuffed to capacity, stuck on the top of a dowel rod, and tied off with a colorful ribbon makes a great pointer for tracking print with big books and reading charts. Kids will love using it!

Since this lesson needs to be repeated often in the beginning of the year, offer variety by inviting a student to come and color the "quiet spaces" between each word of your message with a crayon (or transparency pen). You and the other students can put your fingers to your mouths and make a "shhhh" (quiet!) sound for each space colored.

STEPS

1. Write a Morning Message to students to greet them each day. Let them observe as you write to them. Start with just a couple of sentences in the first weeks of school and progress as students' understanding grows and as their attention spans increase. For example:

   August 15, 2004

   Dear Boys and Girls,
   Today we are going to visit Mrs. Jones in the library. She will show us how we can borrow books to bring back to the class. We can also take her books home with us!

   Love,
   Mrs. Wright

2. As you write, say the words out loud, pausing between each word so that children will be able to make a match between spoken and written language. Share with students that there is always a "quiet space" between every word that is written. Show them where this space is.

3. Use your finger or a pointer to read the message once or twice after you have completed it. Lifting the pointer from the paper should help to emphasize the correspondence between spoken and written language.

4. Again using the pointer, have students count the number of words in each sentence with you. Record the number of words at the end of each sentence. Count the number of "quiet spaces," too. This combines a little math along with language study!

Drawing and writing together

EXPLANATION: To support beginning writers and to build their confidence, model how pictures can be used as a "real" way for some students to tell what they want to say on paper.

SKILL FOCUS

Using pictures and labels to convey meaning

QUICK HINTS

Take cues from your students on writing topics. Write often on whatever subject they love hearing about—your dog, your children, when you were little, or your hobbies. Watch for signs, though, that they're ready to hear about something new. Then it's time to change!

Share with your students that drawing pictures was the earliest way that people wrote about things as a way of communicating. Find pictures of hieroglyphics to show such writing to your class.

STEPS

1. Share with students that you are going to tell them about something by drawing pictures.

2. Talk as you draw simple pictures to represent ideas. For example:

   "Boys and girls, I want to tell you about how my dog lets me know when it's time for a walk every night. Let me draw a picture of myself. (Sketch a stick figure of yourself.) *We'll know that's me because I'm going to write my name beside my picture. Mrs. is written with a capital 'm' and an 'r' and an 's.'* (Write these and the remaining letters of your name.) *Just after supper every night, I hear something jiggling down the hall as I'm finishing the dishes in the kitchen. Guess what it is?* (Begin to sketch a simple picture of a little dog.) *Yes, it's my dog, Mazie. Let me write her name beside her picture.* (Write "Mazie" as you say the names of the letters.) *Mazie is dragging something along in her mouth. Let me add that to my picture and see if you can guess what it is.* (Sketch a leash in the dog's mouth.) *How many of you know what a leash is?* (Call on a student who knows.) *Right! And do you know that Mazie lets me know every night that she's ready for her walk by bringing me her leash? She knows that she can't go walking without it! Isn't she clever?"*

3. Read over the words again, asking children if they remember what these words say.

Stretching to spell

EXPLANATION: Writing provides students with their greatest opportunity to apply their understanding of how phonics works in reading and writing. The encoding process is when students match the necessary sounds and symbols in their minds before putting something on paper. Adults do this automatically, but emergent writers struggle with this skill.

──{ SKILL FOCUS }──

Stretching out sounds to spell phonetically

──{ QUICK HINTS }──

When well-meaning teachers spell words for students as students write, who gets to "show off" what they know? The teacher, that's who! Who really needs to show off what they know about phonics, letters, and sounds? The students do, of course, so let them! Create a comfortable environment where students can approximate spellings without penalty. Find every occasion to encourage their efforts, saying, "You did such a great job of writing down the sounds in that word!"

STEPS

1. Model how to stretch out the sounds of words that you're unsure how to write. For example, in the model below, say the bold-print words out loud very slowly and record only the sounds that are clearly heard:

   *My **grndfathr** had a farm when I was a little girl. In **Awgust**, he would plant a row of seeds for each of his **grndchildrin**. He wrote our names on a sign at the end of our row of seeds. Later in the fall, the seeds would grow into **pumkins**. We each picked the biggest **pumkin** in our row to take home!*

2. Tell students that there will often be words they'll want to use in their writing that they don't know how to write. Tell them that sometimes when you write, you want to use a word you're not sure how to spell. And make sure they know that it's okay to make a good guess.

3. Conclude the lesson by saying, "How could we stretch out the word *dinosaurs* if we want to write about them today?" Write what children offer. "How would we stretch out *helicopter* if we want to write about taking a ride in one?" Again, guide students to stretch out the sounds. "Now, remember that we're going to get our ideas down and make our best guesses about spellings of words today."

Note: In all lessons throughout this book, stretch out difficult or unfamiliar words. You may wish to circle them and comment, "This is how this word sounds to me. I'll check the spelling later if I need to."

Using rime/rhyme to spell

EXPLANATION: When we come to words we're unsure of, we often use a strategy of thinking of words we already know that may have the same sound pattern (rhyme). We use the spelling pattern (rime) of that word and manipulate the beginning or ending to make our new word. This is a useful strategy that students need to learn.

SKILL FOCUS

Using familiar sounds and patterns to spell.

QUICK HINTS

Here's a quick glossary to explain some important words:

Rime: the spelling pattern of a one- or two-syllable word, including all the letters starting with the first vowel of the word.
    Examples:
    brain (rime is "ain")
    pin (rime is "in")

Rhyme: the sound pattern formed either by words with the same spelling patterns or by different spelling patterns that sound alike.
    Examples:
    Brain and *rain*
    Bright and *kite*

STEPS

1. This lesson fits nicely with some of the word study that occurs in your class. If you've been studying word families (rime patterns), brainstorm with your students a list of words that use the same spelling patterns. For example, make a list of the words that have the *ack* pattern that sound like /ack/, such as:

sack	*Jack*	*rack*	*tack*	*whack*
back	*hack*	*lack*	*Mack*	*knack*
pack	*quack*	*Zack*		

2. Make up a silly sentence with your students using some of the words from your list that rhyme, such as:
    Mack put *Zack* in a *sack* on his *back*.
    *The duck went *quack* when he stepped on a *tack*.*

    Underline the spelling patterns in the sentences (as shown above) and read the words out loud together to help both visual and auditory learners.

3. After having some fun with these sentences, tell students that this is also how they can make good guesses at words they want to use in their writing but might not know how to spell. Say, "If I were writing a story about a boy named Zack, I would think about what letters make the /ack/ sound. That would help me put it on paper and would help me be able to read it back."

4. If you're using a Word Wall or word family charts in your class, refer to them frequently for the rime/spelling patterns that you need for other words.

Relying on the room for spelling help

EXPLANATION: The classroom environment can offer much support for students' reading and writing. Word Walls that have high frequency words for quick and easy reference, cluster charts of words that are used frequently, and some pattern word charts/word families are great resources for young readers and writers. Be selective, though, and try not to clutter the room.

SKILL FOCUS

Using resources for spelling

MATERIALS

A print-rich environment, with resources such as word walls, cluster/theme charts, and pictionaries

QUICK HINTS

After modeling this several times, you might play a game of Where's the Word? As you come to a word in your writing, share it aloud with the class and ask if anyone knows where it might be spelled in the room. Give a volunteer a pointer or a flashlight and have him find the word and spell it for you as you write it.

STEPS

1. Begin by saying, "Boys and girls, did you know that we have **helping walls** in our classroom? Let me show you!"

2. Write for the students and stop to use the class resources as you write. Below is what you might say as you write. The teacher's comments are in parentheses; what she writes is in italics.

   (Oh, my very first word is under our calendar!) *Today we are going* (That's on the Word Wall, so I can spell it correctly.) *to art with Mrs. Howell.* (Oh, her name is on our schedule chart!) *She will teach* (That's a word I need to stretch out because it's not on the walls anywhere.) *us about the primary colors* (I can look at our color chart for the word *color* and for these next words, too!) *of red, yellow, and blue. We are going* (That's on the Word Wall again!) *to make pinwheels!*

3. Conclude by saying, "The room was certainly a big help today in my writing! You can use the helping walls when you write every day, too!"

4. If time allows, take a tour of the class to talk about the types of information on the helping walls. Helping walls might have:
   • Color charts
   • Calendars with days and months
   • Pictionaries
   • Cluster charts with content words
   • Word Walls (with high frequency words)
   • Calendar activity words (*today, yesterday, tomorrow*)

Introducing the tools for writing

EXPLANATION: Writers need the right tools to produce a quality product. Students develop confidence as writers when there is a structure and known resources associated with a task. Beginning writing lessons should therefore focus on the tools good writers need.

SKILL FOCUS

Getting started with appropriate materials

QUICK HINTS

Many classrooms have a writing center where paper, pencils, dictionaries, a thesaurus, and publishing materials are stored. Use an old briefcase in the display to help students think of the center as their office.

Use plastic baskets to store pencils, journals, and more. These baskets can be distributed to each table or group of students.

STEPS

1. Make sure that the materials used for writing are organized and available for use so that students do not spend writing time looking for paper and pencil. Inform the class about the procedure to follow when distributing these materials. Early writing may be on unlined paper, then half-and-half paper, and later in some type of notebook. Many teachers organize students by color groups, days of the week, etc., and ask table captains to assist in the distribution of materials.

2. Practice identifying what materials are needed, where they are located, and how they will be distributed. Allow the designated students enough time to practice distributing appropriate materials in an efficient manner.

3. Once students progress through the early stages of writing, establish a method of keeping first drafts together in order to monitor progress over time. Use spiral notebooks, sewn-in composition books, or grade-level writing paper stapled together and kept in a pocket folder.

4. Materials for publishing, such as special markers and unique writing paper, can be stored in a center. Tell the students that these materials are very special and can be used when they are ready to publish one of their writing pieces. This might motivate the child who is reluctant to write enough to publish.

Introducing half-and-half paper

EXPLANATION: After students have spent time using unlined paper to represent their early writing stages, such as "driting" or copying words from the room, introduce half-and-half writing paper. This paper is blank on the top half and lined for writing on the bottom half. Ask students to use it to write words and/or sentences that represent their drawings.

SKILL FOCUS

Using half-and-half paper to write and to illustrate

MATERIALS & RESOURCES

- *Carl* by Alexandra Day or other picture books students have read
- Half-and-half transparency (See Appendix, page 109)
- Half-and-half paper in a wrapped box (wrapping optional)
- Crayons, pencils

QUICK HINTS

New kinds of writing paper, introduced as students move through the stages of writing, help them to get excited about their growth. They will begin to see themselves as writers.

STEPS

1. Motivate students to write by showing excitement about using half-and-half paper for the first time. You might wrap a box of it like a present. Then say: "Today is very special. Can anyone guess what I have in this box?" Unwrap the box and distribute the new writing paper.

2. Share one of Alexandra Day's picture books from the *Carl* series. At some point in the book, have the students predict what might happen next. Model drawing their predicted next scene and then write two or three sentences describing the drawing. This series is very humorous, and children will laugh out loud at Carl's antics. If you make your example silly, students will eagerly draw and write. Continue to brainstorm other possible predictions.

3. Provide crayons for drawing and pencils for writing.

4. On half-and-half paper, ask students to draw in the top half of the paper what they think will happen. Set a timer so that the drawing time is limited. When the timer goes off, direct students to write what they can about their drawing on the lines provided.

Using writing paper with margins

EXPLANATION: After several weeks, most students move from using half-and-half paper or lined paper with no margins to using lined paper with margins. At that point, it is helpful to model how the margins help guide their writing.

SKILL FOCUS

Using margins as a transition to standard lined paper

MATERIALS & RESOURCES

- Transparency of lined paper with margins (See Appendix, page 110)
- Transparencies of student writing on paper with margins
- Pocket chart highlighters (colorful, flexible, vinyl strips)

QUICK HINTS

Children enjoy using different types of writing paper. Using the see-through strip and working with a partner will also motivate them to write.

"Teachers should look for and accommodate young writers' natural patterns of behavior."
—Donald Graves, *The Child, the Writing Process and the Role of the Professional*

STEPS

1. Build excitement with each transition to different types of writing paper by showing transparencies from the year before. Introduce students to writing on paper with margins. Point out how the margin is a guide for the writing.

My dog is two years old. She loves to play with an old leather shoe.

2. With the transparent highlighter strip, align the left edge with the left margin to help students to see how all the words stay to the right of the left margin.

3. Continue to build excitement by giving each child a transparent pocket chart highlighter strip. Remind them to use it to line up their words with the margin as they write on paper with margins.

4. Allow partners time to check each others' writing to be sure that the margin was used correctly.

Legibility

EXPLANATION: If writing is not legible, then none of the conventions or skills that we teach can be assessed, nor can the writing be shared and enjoyed. On most state writing tests, illegible handwriting receives a "0." Students need to understand how important it is for their letter formation and spacing to be legible. Be careful, however, not to emphasize perfection on rough draft writing. Legibility, though, is a must!

SKILL FOCUS

Understand that others must be able to read our writing.

QUICK HINTS

Students who have difficulty with handwriting legibility may find that word processing software makes publishing easier. They will, however, still need to practice handwriting. Offering different writing tools such as colored pencils or erasable pens might encourage them to enjoy their practice.

Allow students who do not space adequately between words to use a physical "spacer," such as a popsicle stick.

STEPS

1. Show students writing that cannot be read. Use anonymous student samples or create your own examples to show letters that are incorrectly formed and spacing that is poor.

2. Tell students, "Boys and girls, when I write the Morning Message or write our stories on the writing charts, I have to be sure that I write the letters, words, and sentences so that you can read what I have to tell you." When students write, ask them to be sure their writing, letter formation, and spacing allows the reader to understand what they are trying to say.

3. As a follow-up after students are all at the writing stage (beyond making pictures and random letters), write student names on popsicle sticks. Ask each student to draw a stick from the stack and write a message to that student.

4. Ask students to look at their handwriting to be sure that it can be read by themselves and others.

5. Later in the year, extend this lesson by assigning students authentic writing tasks. (That's when they'll really care about writing their best!) They might:
   a. Write a note to the art teacher asking what the next art project will be.
   b. Write to the guidance counselor to find out when the next classroom visit will be.
   c. Write to the principal to invite him/her to read a book to the class.
   Remind students to write letters, words, and sentences clearly so that their messages can be read by the person to whom they are writing.

Section Two: Planning for Writing

Beginning writers need to view writing as merely another way of sharing what they want to tell. In fact, as we model writing on most days in the beginning of the year, we start our mini-lesson by saying, "What do I want to tell you today?" Communicating that writing is telling is one of the most important concepts we can teach our youngest, newest writers.

If we were to look at writing as we do speaking, we might realize that we rarely do much more than some "mental

Many students find that writing is much easier if a plan precedes it.

drafting" before the words roll from our lips. We don't stop to map our words or make a written list of the things we might talk about. Much of our planning is done as a mental process. Beginning writing should occur the same way. We merely want the little ones to tell us something—but to "say" it on paper.

Young writers sometimes need to be convinced that they have something worthy of putting on paper. They are familiar with the printed pages of their favorite published books and don't necessarily realize that writing is done for many different purposes and by everyone! Many children come to school first thing in the morning, tugging on our skirts or slacks, saying, "Teacher, I've got something to tell you!" This is a great time to respond, "Oh, I hope you'll tell me about it in your writing today!" Channel this excitement into writing by having students express their everyday thoughts, feelings, and events on paper.

Sometimes teachers need to nudge a bit and give students ideas about what in their everyday lives would make a good topic for writing. Offer statements about your own life—such as "You won't believe what happened when I tried to bake a cake last night" or "I want to tell you something funny my cat did last weekend"—to model the thought process that gets kids started with their writing. They all have something to tell!

The lessons in this section offer different ways of showing students how they might get started writing. The hope is that you'll offer these ideas as options to choose from, rather than requiring students to use them on a regular basis. Many students will initially fear putting pencil to paper just because it's something new and intimidating. Your lessons will provide a level of comfort for them, and will make getting started much less of a "big deal."

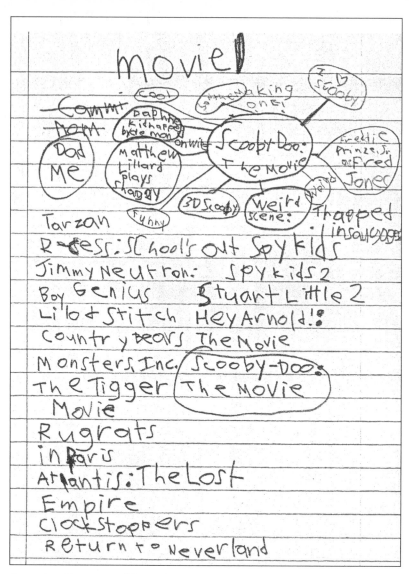

A movie title is moved from the jot list to a web for planning.

Choosing a topic

EXPLANATION: Having background knowledge about a topic is essential for students to be able to write about it. Topics should therefore come from their personal experiences. Much oral rehearsal of "things I could tell you about" should happen before they choose a topic independently.

SKILL FOCUS

Choosing a topic based on personal experience

QUICK HINTS

Remember that, in first grade, most writing during the Writing Workshop is "kids' choice" writing. Even though you model how to use many writing conventions and techniques, your students may or may not apply those immediately. The goal is for them to absorb your lessons and use what they've learned when they're ready.

STEPS

1. Begin by saying to students that you have many things you could tell them about today. Think of three areas of experiences that you could write about—sports, family, pets, etc. Let students know that you will share your experiences through writing all year, then share a topic from each of the three areas: "I could tell about a football game that went into four overtimes, or about my husband's birthday that was a catastrophe, or about my cat that had to be taken to the vet for x-rays after being hit by a car!" Then focus on one of these topics and share a reason for selecting it. For example, "I think I will write about the birthday because in the end we had such a good time and made such a mess!" Then write about the topic on a transparency.

2. Set the timer for five minutes and ask children to share ideas they want to write about with a partner. This will give students ideas that they might not have thought about on their own.

3. As students return to their seats one by one, have each announce their topic. Allow the more fluent readers and writers to go first. This gives more thinking time to the students who are stuck on what to write about.

4. Most of the writing time on this day should be spent in oral rehearsal of ideas to write about. The students will write their topic on their paper. The next day, the lesson might continue with instruction on what to do once a topic is chosen.

Planning before writing

EXPLANATION: Much of the real-life writing that adults do is first-draft writing. Often we need to think through a sequence of events in order to organize our writing. Model the skill of mental planning prior to writing repeatedly throughout the year.

— SKILL FOCUS —

Learning to think about and plan a piece before writing it

— MATERIALS & RESOURCES —

Timer

— QUICK HINTS —

Use a timer in your lessons to help students develop a concept of time and to help you to pace your lessons.

For an additional mini-lesson on mental planning, distribute three sticky notes to each student. Ask them to write one idea about their topic on each sticky note. List their topics on the chalkboard in various places, and let them come and place the sticky notes around their topic.

STEPS

1. After selecting a writing topic, writers think of details they want to include. To model this, continue using the topic you selected in the mini-lesson on choosing a topic. Think aloud about what you will write about. You might say,

   "There are several things I want to include when I write about the birthday party. I want to tell you about the decorations. We had balloons and paper streamers that were red and white. The park shelter was full of balloons and many of them popped before the party was over! Next, I want to tell you about the refreshments. Cake, ice cream, and punch were served. I had so much to eat that I looked like one of the balloons! Another thing I could tell you about is the present I wrapped with special red and white paper and ribbon. It was too beautiful to open. Finally, you have to know about the stray dog that ran through the party and knocked over the food, popped the balloons, and jumped with muddy paws on several of the guests! These are the things I plan to write about. Now I want you to think of details for your own pieces."

2. Invite two or three students to share with the class their writing topic and their plan for writing. Students will get ideas from listening to others describe their plans.

3. Prior to writing, oral discussion is important. Ask students to discuss with a partner what they plan to include in their writing. Set a timer for a few minutes so that each partner has time to share.

Jotting down ideas

EXPLANATION: First graders can eventually move from mental planning to writing their ideas in a list-like format. These lists serve as concrete reminders of things to include in their writing.

SKILL FOCUS

Creating jot list for planning

QUICK HINTS

Model making a list of things to do in order to promote an important real-life skill. Opportunities for this occur naturally throughout the year. Examples of things to list include:

- Books to get from the library
- Supplies needed from the office
- Winners from the PTA fundraiser
- Materials needed for the science experiment

STEPS

1. Tell students: *"Yesterday, I told you about a birthday party. Before I can begin to write, I need to write a few words that will help me to remember what to write about. Writers call these words a 'jot list.'"*

2. Make a list on the overhead as you think aloud: *"I'll start by telling you who the party was for."* Add the name *Mr. Ford* to the beginning of the list.

   "Next, I'll tell you where the party was held." Add *the park* to the jot list.

   "Then I will describe the party." Add *birthday party* to the jot list.

   "I could tell you about the decorations and the food." Add *decorations* and *food* to the jot list.

   "Presents were a part of the party, too." Add *presents* to the jot list. *"The uninvited guest—the dog—should be included, too."*

> **Jot List**
> Mr. Ford
> the park
> birthday party
> decorations
> food
> presents
> the dog

"Now I am ready to begin writing about the party because I have made a list to help me plan."

Mapping an outline

EXPLANATION: Using a visual, such as an outline or other graphic organizer, assists first graders in planning their writing. The visual must be simple so that the image can be recalled. The image will help them mentally plan for writing tasks.

SKILL FOCUS

Using an outline before writing

MATERIALS

- Copy of a handprint
- A garden glove (optional)

QUICK HINTS

Cut a sticky note vertically (up to the sticky part) into five strips. Tell the students to write the 5 Ws on the strips. Ask them to place one strip at a time on their paper and write words on the paper that can match the question on their sticky note.

Who
Mom
Beth
teacher
Rover

STEPS

1. Explain to students that writers can use a simple outline to plan their writing. This outline will remind them of things they can tell about in their writing.

2. Trace your hand on an overhead transparency. On the palm write, "My Writing Plan." On each finger write one of the 5 Ws—who, what, why, when, and where. (A light-colored garden glove could serve as a permanent model for this writing plan.)

3. Trace your hand again and substitute facts for the 5 Ws. For example:
   "I want to tell you about my brother and me when we were little."
   Who: my brother and me
   What: he made me eat chicken feed
   Why: to show that I would do anything he told me to do
   When: in the summer when I was four years old
   Where: on our farm

4. Consider distributing a copy of a blank hand to each child for them to use when planning their writing.

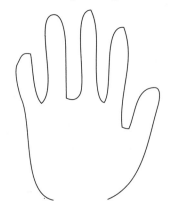

Webbing an outline

EXPLANATION: Like outlines, webs assist beginning writers when planning what to write. Each part of a web represents an idea about a topic.

SKILL FOCUS

Using a web to plan writing

MATERIALS

Drawing paper

QUICK HINTS

The best graphic organizers are the ones that the students draw themselves. Keep the visual simple so that students can reproduce it easily.

At another time, ask students to draw a web of a paragraph from their science book. This activity requires that they "read like a writer."

STEPS

1. Model how writers use a web to plan their writing. Think aloud about what you wish to write about. For example, *"This weekend my daughter, Susan, brought her new pet home to visit. Boy, was I surprised to see a flying squirrel in its cage! I think today I will tell you about Peepers. I will use a web to plan what I want to say."* Talk about each of the ideas as you add them one at a time.

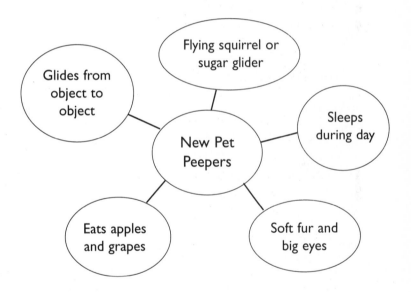

2. Give students time to think of something they want to tell you about.

3. Share examples of topics, such as pets, favorite sports, your church, or a sister or brother.

4. Give students drawing paper to make a web of their plan.

Section Three: Making Writing Cleaner and Clearer (Conventions)

The research on teaching writing is clear: grammar instruction does not automatically cause students to write more correctly (Hillocks and Smith, 2003), and traditional instruction with specific writing assignments and feedback has only small effects (Hillocks, 1986).

This beginning writer uses the room environment for spelling words correctly in his writing.

The Writing Workshop approach has become so popular and has yielded such positive results in part because it places instruction in grammar, mechanics, and usage in a context that makes good sense to students. When those same elements were taught through exercises in a grammar book, students complied with the requests to complete the exercises but often failed to transfer what they'd learned into their own writing. They robotically underlined the subjects with one line and the verbs with two, but they clearly didn't see this as a real-life task. Consequently, they didn't make the connection that each sentence they composed themselves needed to have a subject and a verb, and that the subjects and verbs had to agree with each other. If students fail to see the relevance of what they're asked to do, the transfer of learning to real reading and writing probably won't occur.

Demonstrating in daily writing how and why commas are necessary, why capital letters are needed at the beginning of sentences, and why sentences need subjects and verbs to be complete helps students to see how much clearer writing is when it uses those conventions. And their "buy-in" is therefore quick. When students see how distracting errors are for the reader, they're likely to pay closer attention to cleaning up their own errors before sharing their writing with a peer or with you. And when planning to publish their work and put it on display for others to read, they'll take pride in getting it as error-free as possible.

Don't misunderstand us—we believe that teaching grammar, mechanics, and usage is important. But when teaching first graders, we must not overemphasize correctness during our writing instruction. If we do, our students will quickly get the idea that they can't consider themselves writers until they know all of the things that make writing perfect—plural possessives, verb tenses, introductory phrases and clauses, and so many other elements of correctness.

Instead, we emphasize the notion that writing is telling—a basic means of communication—and that everyone has something to tell. This allows students to see themselves as writers. So start your Writing Workshop daily by asking, "Now what do I want to tell you today?" Concentrate on allowing students to become fluent in their writing, giving them the fundamentals of written communication. Then—and only then—gradually begin to teach them the more technical aspects of writing.

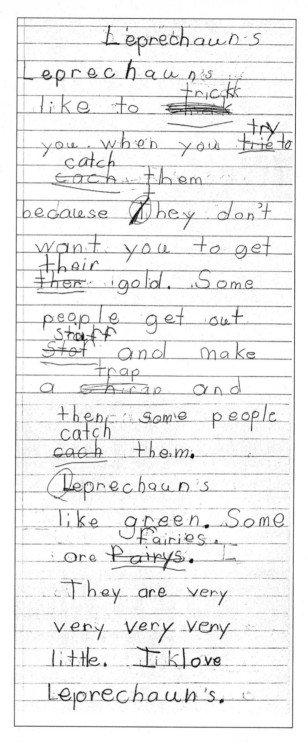

As this student corrects errors, he makes his first draft cleaner.

Writing sentences

EXPLANATION: Writing effective sentences is an essential skill for successful communication. Young writers need extensive practice in this area in order to develop. In this lesson we show how sentences express complete thoughts.

SKILL FOCUS

Understanding that a sentence expresses a complete thought

MATERIALS

- Markers in two colors
- Classroom objects such as board games, pencil holder, SSR basket, Unifix cubes, puppet, wind chimes, paper maché art, a green plant

QUICK HINTS

During individual student conferences, work with students on identifying complete sentences in a piece of their own writing. Have them find the "who" and "what" of the sentence and then together look for the "action."

STEPS

1. Model writing sentences that describe an object in the classroom. Include two incomplete sentences. For example:

   The Crayon Box
   The box of crayons is small. There are 8 crayons in the box. The crayons are brand new. The black crayon. All of the crayons have sharp points. And paper covers. We use the crayons when we draw.

2. Explain that a sentence must express a complete thought. Discuss each sentence in the example and identify the two incomplete sentences. Underline the complete sentences with one color and the incomplete sentences with the other color marker.

3. Ask students to add words to change the two incomplete sentences into complete ones. For example:
   "The black crayon is my favorite.
   "They all have paper covers."

To extend this activity:

Focused: Put a classroom object at each table. Tell students to write sentences with complete thoughts to describe the objects at their tables. Have several students share what they have written.

Self-selected: Have the students write on a topic of their choice. Allow a few minutes at the conclusion of the writing time for students to read each of their sentences to see if they all are complete and make sense.

Sentences have subjects and verbs

EXPLANATION: Beginning writers need an understanding of the basic ingredients of a complete sentence. In the previous lesson we focused on the fact that a sentence expresses a complete idea; now we introduce that a sentence has a subject and a verb. With beginning writers, keep your presentation of these ingredients as simple as possible. Getting too technical may inhibit them.

— SKILL FOCUS —

Sentences have subjects and verbs

— MATERIALS —

Prepared piece of writing

— QUICK HINTS —

As a follow-up to this lesson on subjects and verbs, compose a simple story on the board or on a chart. Leave out the subjects and verbs. On tagboard or segments of sentence strips, write many possible choices of subjects and verbs for the missing spaces. Let children volunteer to come up and tape their choices in the spaces. If subjects and verbs are placed appropriately, allow the choices to be silly sometimes!

STEPS

1. Say to students: "Today I have a piece of writing to share that's a big mystery. Something is wrong with it, and I hope you can solve the mystery and help me read it!" Share:
   Hickory, dickory, dock.
   *** ran up the clock.   *** stuck one.   *** ran down.
   Hickory, dickory, dock.

2. Children who have come to your class with a history of nursery rhymes will know what's missing in these sentences. Let them help you fill in the missing words.

3. Tell students that it's important in their writing to have a complete sentence. These sentences didn't have a subject. We didn't know at first who "ran" or what "stuck."

4. Write a short paragraph of your own, and let students decide if each sentence is complete. Try to use sentences with action verbs, as below:
   We walked to the fire station yesterday. Held hands and sang songs on the way. At the station we climbed on the fire truck. The firemen talked to us about their jobs. We had fun!

5. Read each sentence aloud with the students and discuss whether the sentence has everything it needs to be complete and to sound right. The second sentence needs a subject, someone or something that is holding hands and singing. Add the subject and read the sentence aloud.

6. A similar lesson can be used for verbs that are missing. Have fun practicing with students so that they develop a sense of what sounds right and complete.

Subject and verb agreement

EXPLANATION: All students must develop their knowledge of syntax, especially those who haven't had the advantage of hearing proper syntax in their home environment. They need the ability to recognize what sounds right and what is right in standard English usage. Remember that you constantly provide models of good syntax for your students as you speak, write, and read.

SKILL FOCUS

Recognize that subjects and verbs must agree in sentences

MATERIALS

- Flip chart
- Sentence strips or tagboard
- Tape or glue

QUICK HINTS

This lesson on subject-verb agreement can also be made into a center activity. Package sentence strips with missing words, along with an envelope containing a choice of words to fit into the empty spaces. Let students practice picking the best choice based on their understanding of subjects and verbs.

STEPS

1. Say to students: "Today I have a writing puzzle for you! I have a paragraph that's missing some words, and I want you to help me solve the puzzle of the missing words."

2. Reveal the following piece of writing or a similar one of your own design on a flip chart. Have the missing verbs written on sections of sentence strips or tagboard.

Sassy and Freckles

Sassy and Freckles ____ cats. They ____ always playing together. If Sassy __ frisky, then Freckles __ frisky, too. If Freckles __ sleepy, then Sassy __ sleepy. They ___ copycats!

3. Show the class that you have the missing words on separate pieces of sentence strips or tagboard. Discuss with them which words fit in which spaces. What are the clues that can help you make the right choices? In your discussion, point out that the word *are* is always used when you're talking about both characters. The word *is* is used when one character is mentioned.

4. Be sure students realize that the same rule applies to these verbs when you're talking about people rather than cats! Remind students that we make these kinds of choices every day as we speak and as we write.

Capitals at beginning of sentences

EXPLANATION: One of the writing conventions that children learn first is that sentences must begin with capital letters. Be sure to reserve this lesson until students have developed familiarity with uppercase letters. They should feel comfortable with writing before they have to pay attention to conventions.

SKILL FOCUS

Uppercase letters are always used at the beginning of sentences.

MATERIALS

- "Stop" sign made of red construction paper
- "Go" sign made of green construction paper

QUICK HINTS

Remember that students learn best in different ways. Be cognizant of their diverse learning styles and try to design activities that allow for visual, auditory, kinesthetic, and tactile experiences. Accordingly, follow-up activities for this lesson might include having students march in place as you track print—starting as you point to the capital letters and stopping at the end punctuation.

STEPS

1. Lead children in a march around the room or in some brief physical activity. Tell them that, just like drivers in cars, they are to pay attention to the "stop" and "go" signs. When you hold up the red sign, they should quickly stop. When you hold up the green sign, they can go.

2. After a short period of trying this activity, settle students down for your mini-lesson. Share with them that writers must read signs just like drivers do. Explain that every sentence has a stop and go sign. The go sign is a capital letter, which lets us know that the sentence is starting. The end mark signals that the sentence is coming to a stop and that a complete thought or idea has been expressed. Briefly share with students that there are different kinds of stop signs, including periods, exclamation points, and question marks. (These will be covered more specifically in later lessons.)

3. Provide a composition, such as the following:
   Mrs. Harris is our cafeteria director. She plans healthy meals for us. She has to think about all of the foods that are good for us. She cares about us and wants us to grow strong. We are lucky to have Mrs. Harris at our school!

4. Work on your composition together with students, asking them to help highlight the capitals in green and the end punctuation marks in red.

5. End the lesson by saying, "Think about your writing today. Are you giving the right stop and go signals?"

Capitals for names of people

EXPLANATION: Beginning writers learn that capital letters are used at the beginning of sentences and for proper nouns. Writing the names of people is the easiest application of this convention for them. The use of capitals with places and things can be modeled regularly, although holding students accountable for it at this point may be a bit too demanding.

SKILL FOCUS

Using capital letters with names of people

MATERIALS

- Display of students' names with correct use of capital letters in each
- Individual letters of one student's name printed on a transparency and then cut apart
- A large capital letter for each student's first name (use colored marker on half sheets of white paper to make these)

QUICK HINTS

Students can quickly learn letters and sounds if instruction helps them make close associations between them. Try teaching by exploring the names of all class members.

STEPS

1. Start by saying, "Today you are all going to be detectives to help me solve a mystery. We have a mystery student and we must figure out who it is. We have all of the letters of the student's name, but the letters are scrambled." Spread the letters out on the overhead projector in random fashion.

2. Ask if anyone notices any clues among the letters. Guide students to notice the one capital letter that begins the name. Then let them explore the different student names that begin with that letter and help them narrow their guesses.

3. Once students have used their deductive reasoning to figure out the correct name, help them generalize that all students' names begin with capital/upper-case letters. Tell them that everyone is important, and that we all deserve a capital letter! Prepare a capital letter for each student. Ask the class to say the letter as you show it. Then tell them that if their name starts with that letter, they can come and get the letter. (Be sure to make multiple copies for students whose names start with the same letter!)

4. Show students how we have to remember the important letters as we write about people. Write an example such as:
   We are all special! Our names all start with capital letters to show how special we are. John and Jessica have names that start with the same letter. Abbie's name is at the beginning of the alphabet, and Zack's name is at the end. Our names are all special!

5. After reading back through your writing, have students tell you the reason for each capitalized letter in it.

Capitals for names of places and things

EXPLANATION: After learning that names and sentences begin with capital letters, beginning writers are ready to learn that other proper nouns—places and things—begin with capital letters, too. Model this regularly, but holding students accountable for it is probably asking too much of them at this stage.

SKILL FOCUS

Using capital letters with proper nouns (names of places/things)

MATERIALS

Environmental print from various food products

QUICK HINTS

An easy class book to make in the beginning of the year—one that all students can read—is a book of environmental print. Use the products from the lesson on this page (cereal and noodle boxes, fast food bags, etc.). Flatten the packages or bags, punch a hole in the top left corners, and string them on a large silver ring clasp. Make a colorful cover, and watch students have fun reading! They might enjoy taking this book home to read to parents early in the year!

STEPS

1. Write this sentence for the class: We are celebrating birthdays today for Brian and Moy! Then ask: "Boys and girls, remind me why I need an uppercase letter for *We, Brian,* and *Moy.*"

2. Tell students: "Today we're going to learn more ways to use uppercase letters. Capitals are used for special words—like names!"

3. Show students some product containers, such as a cereal box, a bag from a local fast food company, and a placemat with a restaurant's name on it. Tell them that these are the special names of things and places, just like "Nancy" is the special name of a girl. Explain that when we write the name of a special person, place, or thing, we start it with a capital letter. Show them the difference between ordinary or plain and special by making a list on the board, such as:

The plain word	*The special word*
(no capital letter)	*(capital letter)*
girl	*Nancy*
teacher	*Mrs. Wright*
cereal	*Crunchies*
city	*Columbia*

4. Next, show your students how this concept works in the context of writing. For example:

   The name of our school is Learnit Elementary School in a city called Columbia. Our principal is Mrs. Mixon. She tells us that we are special people. We are all proud of our school.

5. Ask students why *Learnit Elementary School, Columbia,* and *Mrs. Mixon* are all capitalized. Ask them why *school, city,* and *principal* are not capitalized. Clarify as necessary.

Using periods

EXPLANATION: Young writers are often confused about how to use ending punctuation in their writing. Oral conversation has been their predominant means of communication. Suddenly they are asked to write down their ideas in words and sentences, and must use ending punctuation to ensure that their writing makes sense.

SKILL FOCUS

Using periods for complete sentences

MATERIALS

- Colored markers
- Red crayons

QUICK HINTS

Draw a red period on several tongue depressors. (Red is for "stop.") Give one to each student. Ask students to hold up the tongue depressors at the end of each statement that is read or spoken aloud.

Give students a paragraph of three to five sentences. Omit the periods and tell them to add a period at the end of a complete thought.

STEPS

1. Have one student tell in several sentences about an event—going to the circus, learning to swim, etc. Ask the other students to listen carefully and to raise their hands after they hear a complete statement. For example:

   "I got a shiny, new bike for Christmas (raise hand) *It was red with chrome handlebars* (raise hand) *My dad helped me ride on the driveway* (raise hand) *At first I was a little shaky* (raise hand) *I got better at keeping the bike steady after more practice* (raise hand) *Now I spend hours and hours riding my bike"* (raise hand)

2. Record each sentence on a chart or transparency. Place a period at the end of each statement where the class raised their hands. (Use a red marker.)

3. Reinforce how the use of a period at the end of a statement helps the reader know when to pause or stop reading.

4. Give each of your students a red crayon or pencil. Ask them to write two or three statements describing an object of their choice and to use the red crayon to make the period at the end of each statement.

Using question marks

EXPLANATION: Students must understand how questions differ from statements and that questions end with a special mark. We often pose questions to help us plan and write nonfiction, so this lesson uses nonfiction.

SKILL FOCUS

Using question marks with "asking" sentences

MATERIALS

• Colored markers
• Green crayons

QUICK HINTS

Draw green question marks on several tongue depressors. Give one to each student to keep with their tongue depressors with periods. Read questions and statements together. Ask students to hold up the tongue depressor with the appropriate ending punctuation.

STEPS

1. Introduce students to the 5 Ws—who, what, when, where, and why—and explain that effective pieces of writing often answer all of these questions. Tell students that posing these five questions can help them plan their writing. Together, generate questions about an animal and write them on a chart or transparency. For example:

   Animal: penguin
   Questions: What do they eat?
   Where do they live?
   Why are they mostly black and white?
   When do they sleep?

2. Write the question marks in a different color than that used for the question. Explain that questions need answers and that the special ending punctuation tells the reader to look for an answer later in text.

3. List four different animals. Ask students to pick one and write a list of questions about what they would like to find out about the animal. Ask them to write the question marks with a green crayon.

4. Pair up students. Have them read their questions to each other. Ask them to make sure that the correct ending punctuation is used.

Using exclamation marks

EXPLANATION: Young writers love using this punctuation mark—in this lesson, we introduce the ways the exclamation point is used to help the reader understand the emotion the writer is trying to convey.

SKILL FOCUS

Using exclamation marks to convey surprise, excitement, or emphasis

MATERIALS

- Picture book that includes several exclamation marks
- Colored markers
- Blue crayons

QUICK HINTS

Draw a blue exclamation mark on several tongue depressors. Give these to students to add to the two tongue depressors made for the previous lessons. Read regular statements, questions, and statements that express excitement. Ask students to hold up the appropriate ending punctuation.

STEPS

1. Read a short selection from a book in which exclamation marks are used. With your voice, show how the author intends for the statement of surprise or excitement to be read.

2. Write a paragraph with sentences using periods, question marks, and exclamation marks. Use a different color marker for the three different types of ending punctuation. For example:

The Barn Fire
Have you ever seen a barn burn down? When I was six, I saw my granddaddy's barn burn to the ground. It happened at 9:00 at night. Boy, it was a scary sight!

3. Ask students to write about an exciting topic and to use the exclamation mark appropriately. Give them a blue crayon to make the exclamation marks. Suggest topics, such as falling down on roller skates, the first time jumping off the diving board at the swimming pool, riding the Ferris wheel at the state fair, building a snowman, or performing in a dance recital.

4. Allow students time to read their sentences aloud. Remind them to read the sentences with exclamation marks with surprise or excitement. Over time, help students understand that exclamation marks should be used sparingly in our writing.

Quick editing of first drafts

EXPLANATION: Students need to know basic criteria for their rough-draft writing so that they can make it easier to read back and easier to share with others. Hold them accountable for only a few basic editing criteria. If you choose too many, chances are that students won't use these basics routinely. Keep it simple throughout the year!

SKILL FOCUS

Apply simple criteria to edit first drafts

MATERIALS

Poster board or chart paper

QUICK HINTS

To make the Quick Check list easily accessible to all students, purchase inexpensive plexiglass frames for each cooperative group of students. Type the list on your computer and print copies to display in frames on each table during writing time.

Quick Check List

1. I have my name and date on the paper.
2. I've started every sentence with a capital letter.
3. I've ended each sentence with a ., !, or ?.
4. My sentences all make sense.
5. I've stayed on topic.
6. I've checked my spelling.

STEPS

1. Prior to this mini-lesson, sit down and make a list of the basic criteria that you feel would help students clean up their rough-draft writing each day. You should have around six items on this "Quick Check" list. Remember that this list shouldn't include everything students need in a published piece—only what they need in their rough drafts. (See Quick Hints for a suggested list.)

2. Introduce your Quick Check items one at a time as you feel students are ready for them. Address each item in a mini-lesson and then display the item on a poster in the class. Once it's added to the poster, hold your writers accountable for that item and allow a few minutes at the end of students' writing time for them to use the Quick Check list. After you finish your own model writing pieces, you might model use of the Quick Check list in this way:

   "Now that I've finished writing, boys and girls, help me use the Quick Check list today. Have I remembered to put my name and date on my paper? I surely did! Let me give myself a check on the top of my paper to show that I checked that item. Did I start every sentence with a capital letter? Oops! Here's a sentence that doesn't start with a capital. Let me change that and then I'll give myself a check at the top."

3. If you place one checkmark at the top of your paper for each item and require students to do the same, this process will soon become natural. Students will internalize basic criteria for their rough-draft writing and use them each time they write.

Using singular and plural nouns

EXPLANATION: First graders need a basic understanding of how nouns change a form representing one item to a form representing two or more items. Start simply with the nouns that only require that "s" be added. Later lessons can include "es" endings and irregular changes of words like *mouse* to *mice*, as well as words such as *deer*, which remains *deer*. There's so much to learn!

—(SKILL FOCUS)—

Using singular and plural nouns

—(QUICK HINTS)—

Speaking of doubles… Try binding two or more colored pencils together with rubber bands and placing them in your writing center. Kids will have fun experimenting with this unique writing tool. It makes great designs for art, too!

STEPS

1. Write a simple piece that allows you to use both the singular and plural forms of the same word, as well as some other singular and plural nouns. For example:

   Double Trouble

   *Once upon a time I had just one **dog**. Mazie had her **bed** beside mine She loved to eat out of her **bowl** under my **table**. She met me at the **door** every day when I came home.*

   *Now I have two **dogs**, and things have changed! Now there are two dog **beds** beside mine. Both **dogs** have **bowls** under my table. Both **dogs** greet me at the **door**!*

   *One thing is for sure. Although there's double trouble with two **dogs**, there's also double the love from them!*

2. Underline some of the nouns that refer to people, places, and things. (The ones in bold above are good ones to use.)

3. Make a chart like the one below. List the first underlined word from the passage and ask the students to help you figure how many items are referred to with that word. List other nouns in the same way.

How many?	1	2	more than 2
dog	√		
bed	√		
bowls		√	

4. Let students help you draw a conclusion about what the words have in common: the nouns with "s" at the end represent more than one (plural nouns), and the nouns without an "s" represent only one (singular nouns).

Quotation marks with dialogue

EXPLANATION: Students are exposed to dialogue and the use of quotations in many of the books that they read and in books that are read to them. They are also usually familiar with the less sophisticated but visually effective style of writing dialogue in comics, which use dialogue bubbles. Dialogue bubbles can help students make the transition to using dialogue in their own writing.

SKILL FOCUS

Using quotation marks to convey dialogue

MATERIALS & RESOURCES

- Simple, short comic strip reproduced onto a transparency
- Some good books that model the use of quotation marks, such as *May I Go Out?* by Erin Rosenberg and *The Crayon Box that Talked* by Shane DeRolf

QUICK HINTS

In subsequent lessons, point out that dialogue helps us feel that we're in the story listening to the characters. Invite students to look at their writing to see where having characters talk might be a good idea. Don't overemphasize correct punctuation of dialogue for beginning writers!

STEPS

1. Transfer a simple, short (and, with any luck, funny!) comic strip onto a transparency. Be sure that the strip is one that first graders can relate to. (This might be a regular strip from the newspaper.)

2. Read the comic strip to and with your students. Tell them that you'd like to write about the action in the strip and that you'd like to show them how to write what people say using special marks called quotation marks.

3. Start with the first frame of the comic strip. Retell the frame by writing the exact words that the characters say in quotations, using "he said/she said" references, such as:
   "Why are you sleeping in the afternoon?" Dennis said to Mr. Wilson.
   "I'm just resting my eyes," Mr. Wilson replied from his hammock.

4. If some frames don't use dialogue, simply write the narrative to match the picture.

5. When you're finished with your retelling, read over the piece with your students. Have them notice that the exact words in the comic bubbles are the ones that get the special quotation marks or "talk marks" around them. Show your students how the marks curve around (or hug) the words to make opening and ending quotation marks.

Abbreviating titles

EXPLANATION: Young writers often use people as the subject of their writing. Therefore, it is important for these students to know how to use simple abbreviations for titles of people.

SKILL FOCUS

Using abbreviations with titles: Mr., Mrs., Ms., and Dr.

MATERIALS

• Colored markers
• Chart paper
• Crayons

QUICK HINTS

As a fun activity, list the names of the boys in the class in a column on the board and girls' names in another column. Allow each child to come up and choose a "grown-up" title for themselves. Boys will choose *Mr.* or *Dr.* and girls will choose *Mrs., Ms.,* or *Dr.* Have them write the abbreviations in front of their names.

STEPS

1. Tell the class that you are going to make a list of names of important people in your school. These names will be used in a class story about the school. As you write the names, use the abbreviations *Mr., Mrs., Ms.* and *Dr.* Explain how these abbreviations are short forms for the titles. Write the abbreviations in a different color marker than the last name. For example, your list might include:

   Dr. Davis, the principal
   Mrs. White, the secretary
   Mr. Mendez, the PE teacher
   Ms. Jones, the first-grade teacher
   Mr. Plyler, the third-grade teacher
   Dr. Bell, the music teacher

2. Ask students to choose a person and write several sentences about that person. Give them a crayon to circle an abbreviated title each time it is used.
   Example of student writing:
   Dr. Bell is my music teacher. She lets me sing. We have fun in her class. Our class and Mrs. Jones's class were part of her play. Dr. Bell helped us sing and dance!

3. Use several of the sentences written by students in a class story about important people in your school. Write each abbreviated title in a different color.

Abbreviating months and days

EXPLANATION: First-grade classes work all year with calendar activities in which the months of the year and days of the week are abbreviated. A mini-lesson that focuses on transferring these skills to students' own writing helps them learn to use these abbreviations themselves.

SKILL FOCUS

Using abbreviations for months and days

QUICK HINTS

Make cards with the months and days written out on one side and the abbreviations on the other. Put these in a center for extra practice.

Allow students to abbreviate the date when writing it on daily classwork and writing assignments.

STEPS

1. Use abbreviations for months and days as you model writing a to-do list. For example:

Our Class Activity List for Indoor Recess

Dec.	*Mon.*	*Board Games*
	Tues.	*Musical Chairs*
	Wed.	*Puzzles*
	Thurs.	*Videos*
	Fri.	*CDs*
Jan.	*Mon.*	*Seven-Up*
	Tues.	*Blocks*
	Wed.	*Four Corners*
	Thurs.	*Sing Along*
	Fri.	*Math Games*
Feb.	*Mon.*	*Art Activity*
	Tues.	*Reading Center*
	Wed.	*Cut and Paste*
	Thurs.	*Free Choice*
	Fri.	*Spelling Games*

2. Ask your students to write an activity plan that they would like you to consider for March using abbreviations for the month and the days.

3. Give them a form with three columns to insert the abbreviated month, days, and activities.

Month	Day	Activity
Mar.	Mon.	

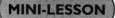

Using the pronouns *I*, *me* and *my*

EXPLANATION: The most important person to a first grader is him- or herself. The first-person narrative is therefore the easiest form of writing at this age, because that writing is all about "me." The words *I*, *me*, and *my* are used many times in this type of narrative, so a mini-lesson on the correct use of these pronouns is necessary.

SKILL FOCUS

Understand the use of the pronouns *I*, *me* and *my*

QUICK HINTS

Read aloud many good examples of personal narratives. Students must hear the words *I*, *me*, and *my* used correctly to be able to determine what "sounds right."

Suggested follow-up:
Write the corrected sentences from "My Bicycle" (at right) on sentence strips. Cut these words apart. Ask students to put the sentences back together using *I*, *me*, and *my* in the correct places.

STEPS

1. Model writing a simple personal narrative which uses *I* and *me* frequently. Intentionally, use the pronouns incorrectly in a few places so that your students can apply the rule of using *I* in the nominative case and *me* in the objective case. (Just don't use these terms with your students!) For example:

    My Bicycle

    I got my first bicycle when I was six years old. My parents gave it to me. Me liked the shiny, red color. Me rode the bicycle up and down the sidewalk. My parents gave I a horn for the handlebars. Me beeped the horn every time me rode the bike. It was fun. I asked my parents to give I a bicycle basket for me books. One day, I fell off my bicycle. Me scraped my knee. Ouch!! I will be more careful next time.

2. Lead the class in reading the narrative aloud. Most of your students will recognize the errors because the sentences don't sound right. It isn't important to emphasize at this time the use of *I* as a subject, *me* as a direct object, or *my* as a possessive. Just make the corrections together.

3. Look for the correct use of *I, me* and *my* as students write personal narratives. During individual conferences, point out how these words are used correctly or incorrectly.

Pronoun agreement

EXPLANATION: Beginning writers experiment with the use of pronouns to replace the names of people, places, and things in their writing. At first, they may have some difficulty picking just the right pronoun. Mini-lessons on pronoun agreement will teach students how to make their decisions.

SKILL FOCUS

Pronoun agreement

MATERIALS

Colored markers

QUICK HINTS

As a follow-up, write sentences using your students' names on chart paper. Don't use pronouns as you normally would. Instead, write sentences such as, "Amanda brought Amanda's lunch to school today." Write different pronouns on note cards, one per card. Hand out the cards to students. Ask them if anyone has a word card that will make the sentences sound better. Have them bring it up and hold it over the word they want to replace. Once you agree that it sounds right, tape the note card over the word.

STEPS

1. After you've taught lessons about what pronouns are, model writing a piece using nouns and pronouns. For example:
   I went to the **zoo** last week. It is such a great place to visit! My **daughter**, **Caroline**, went with me. She loves to watch the **gorillas** play. We went to see them as soon as we arrived. They kept coming to the window to get a look at Caroline's **purse**. It was a bright red color that they liked! We had a great time!

2. With your students, go back and highlight some of the nouns in your passage in one color (such as the ones that are in bold print above).

3. Again with students' help, hunt for the pronouns that took the place of your nouns and underline them with another color (like the ones underlined above).

4. Recreate the chart below on your chalkboard or transparency and fill in several of the people, places, and things that you used in your writing. Point out that only certain pronouns work with certain nouns, and why.

Nouns	Pronouns We Might Use Instead
Mrs. Lovett	I, me, my
Caroline (daughter)	she
zoo	it
gorillas	they, them, their
purse	it
Mrs. L. and Caroline	we

5. If time allows, reread your original piece using just the nouns and no pronouns to remind students again how redundant it sounds.

Apostrophes in contractions

EXPLANATION: Beginning writers enjoy experimenting with contractions, the words that represent our everyday way of speaking. This lesson translates the concept of contractions into a hands-on learning experience.

SKILL FOCUS

Using apostrophes with contractions

QUICK HINTS

As a follow-up activity, make flip cards for each student by following the directions in the Appendix (page 111). Students will enjoy manipulating the cards as they practice with contractions. Besides addressing visual and tactile learners, this activity emphasizes that the apostrophe takes the place of some of the letters when the two words are combined.

STEPS

1. Model a piece of writing that allows you to use words that can be combined into contractions. For example:

   Today we are going to make bird feeders. We will gather pinecones during recess. We will spread peanut butter on the pinecones. Then we will sprinkle birdseed on top of that. I will help you put a hook on the top to hang your feeder. We will put the birdfeeders outside of our window to watch the birds get their food.

2. Read back over what you have written and share, "I want to show you something about my writing and how what I've written is different from the way I might say those same words." Show students how you could change certain words to make them sound more like how we might say them.

3. Here's the revision:

   *Today **we're** going to make bird feeders. **We'll** gather pinecones during recess. **We'll** spread peanut butter on the pinecones. Then **we'll** sprinkle birdseeds on top of that. **I'll** help you put a hook on the top to hang your feeder. **We'll** put the birdfeeders outside of our window to watch the birds get their food*

4. Explain to the class: "These new words that I made by putting two words together and using a mark called an apostrophe (write this for them) are called contractions (write this word for them). We can't do this with all words, though—only certain pronouns and verbs."

5. Use the follow-up activity in the Quick Hints section to give students hands-on experience with contractions.

Using a dictionary

EXPLANATION: Beginning writers need to be introduced to the dictionary as a valuable tool to use during the revision and editing stages of writing. Dictionaries for beginning writers are fun to explore and may even become kids' favorite book in the classroom. Introduce it as you would any other wonder-filled book!

SKILL FOCUS

Knowing how and when to use a dictionary

RESOURCES

Dictionaries for beginning writers, such as: *American Heritage Picture Dictionary, Children's Visual Dictionary,* and *Scholastic First Dictionary*

QUICK HINTS

Help students make the transition to regular use of dictionaries by having them create a personal dictionary. Their dictionary might contain words that are familiar, high frequency words, pattern words, or just neat words that they like. Cutting a composition book (marble book) in half works well, giving students plenty of room to add an entire alphabet of words.

STEPS

1. This is a great activity to do daily to help explore letters, sounds, alliteration, and the dictionary. To start, tell students you're going to have fun with names and learn to use a very important book. Choose a student volunteer and have him or her sit with you in front of the class. Let the student hold the dictionary that you'd like your students to use.

2. Explain to students that the words in a dictionary help them check spellings and tell them the different meanings of words that they might want to use in their writing. Often there are pictures to help explain the words, too. Be sure that students understand that the dictionary is arranged in alphabetical order.

3. In this activity, you'll build a tongue twister around the volunteer's name, using the dictionary to find some good words that start with the beginning letter of his or her name. Ask the class what letter this student's name starts with. Then help your volunteer locate that section of the dictionary.

4. With student input, find some good words in that section for the tongue twister and jot them down. For example, for "r" you might choose *race, run, rock, relay, reel,* or *relish.*

5. Work with the class to write a tongue twister sentence based on some of the words found. For a student named Ray, you might write:
   Ray runs relay races.

6. If you do this daily, you might ask each student to illustrate his or her sentence on art paper. Gradually you'll create a class book of tongue twisters with all of their names!

Section Four: Making Writing Better (Revisions)

Think of your favorite novel, a story that just blew you away, or a non-fiction author that writes prose that is as riveting as a thriller. You don't remember how commas were placed, or that the dialogue was set off with quotation

A teacher-student revision conference.

A student revises her writing.

marks. You recall the voice, the original insights and flow of ideas, the word choice, the cadence of the sentences. These are the qualities that matter. Sure, conventions are important, but the correctness they bring writing are just the window dressing—it's the view through the window, the writing itself, that counts.

Indeed, most writing teachers tell us they'd much prefer to have students who lack the skills of conventions—grammar, mechanics, usage—but who have personality or voice in their writing, who know how to organize their thoughts, and who can develop their ideas with rich, concrete details.

If you've been in the classroom for a few years, think back on the typical What-I-Did-On-My-Summer-Vacation essays that were required of students each September. They were deadly for many of us to read! Most were uninspired, unimaginative, and uncreative (and of course, it wasn't the students' fault, they had never been shown the qualities of good writing). There would occasionally be a paper that stood out from the rest, where a student interjected humor, concrete details, and some enthusiasm. Those pieces glistened like gems amidst the other compositions. This is the kind of writing we are after, and the mini-lessons in this section help you inspire and guide your students toward this level of writing. So what do we mean by making writer better? Revising our work so that it's memorable. So that it has personality, vividness, voice, compelling ideas. You'll be amazed by what your first graders can do with revision. So, without further ado, let's produce papers with personality!

A student has thought through the organization of his piece and drawn an arrow marking his thoughts.

Painting a picture with describing words

EXPLANATION: To learn to use describing words, beginning writers need to hear many books read aloud to them that are rich in adjectives. They also need to brainstorm many describing words on charts in the room, and to see their teacher writing often with describing words.

SKILL FOCUS

Learning to use adjectives, or "describing words"

MATERIALS

• Markers
• Highlighting tape

QUICK HINTS

Some struggling writers will add more detail to their writing if allowed to draw their topic before starting to write about it. Confer with individual students about their descriptive writing. If descriptive words are sparsely used, challenge them to draw a picture to go with their writing and then to add more to the drawing. Finally, ask them to add words to their writing to reflect what they added to the drawing.

STEPS

1. Draw an outline of a cat on the chalkboard or chart. Write a simple sentence describing the cat:
   Butterscotch is my pet kitten.

2. Discuss how you could add to the drawing to show details about the cat. For example, draw fur and color the cat yellow.

3. Next, show how you can add describing words to the sentence:
   Butterscotch is my soft, furry kitten. She is the color of butterscotch candy.

4. Continue adding to the drawing and then writing more describing words and sentences.
   Her whiskers are gray and prickly. She likes to play with a striped red ball. My kitten is great!

5. With a colored marker or highlighter tape, mark the describing words that help the reader visualize the cat.

6. As your students write their descriptions, tell them to remember to paint a picture with describing words.

7. As a follow-up partner activity, have students draw a picture of their partner's descriptive writing. Share the drawings and note details.

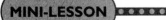

Combining sentences

EXPLANATION: Much of beginning writing consists of short, choppy sentences of three to five words. Later in the year, many students begin starting their sentences with *And*. At this point, a mini-lesson on combining sentences is appropriate.

SKILL FOCUS

Combining sentences for variety

QUICK HINTS

When student writing includes three to five sentences, ask students to count the words in each sentence and write the number in the margin. Challenge them to add to any sentences that are too short and choppy. This increases their awareness of the length of their sentences.

STEPS

1. Model writing a brief paragraph with sentences that are short and choppy. Begin some sentences with the word *And*. You might choose to write about a Science or Social Studies topic. For example:

   The Weather
   Sometimes our weather is perfect. In the spring it is warm. And in the spring it is breezy. The summertime is hot. It is sticky. The fall season is cool. And the fall season is rainy. In the wintertime we have lots of snow. The weather is not pleasant during this season. We have different kinds of weather, and I like it all!

2. Ask the class to help you combine sentences so that they're not short and choppy:

   The Weather
   Sometimes our weather is perfect. In the spring it is warm and breezy. The summertime is hot and sticky. The fall season is cool and rainy. In the wintertime we have lots of snow. The weather is not pleasant during this season. We have different kinds of weather, and I like it all!

3. Have the students select a previous first draft of their own. Help them revise by combining some of their sentences.

Using sparkle words

EXPLANATION: Most primary Health or Science curricula include the study of the five senses. Transferring this study to the students' writing will aid in their retention of this content—and benefit their writing, too. Include read-alouds about the five senses.

SKILL FOCUS

Using sensory details

MATERIALS

- Chart paper
- Sparkle stones or stickers
- Apples

QUICK HINTS

Decorate the "Sparkle Words" chart (see Steps) with little craft stones that sparkle. Stickers that sparkle also make the chart fun to use. Teachers and students should collect "sparkle words" throughout the year. Write them on strips of paper and add to a container that has been covered with glittery paper. During writing time, have students draw words from the container to use in their writing.

STEPS

1. Brainstorm describing words for each of the five senses and list them on a chart. Label the chart "Sparkle Words" since they make our writing "sparkle."

taste	_smell_	_see_	_hear_	_touch_
sweet	clean	clear	loud	smooth
sour	burned	foggy	soft	bumpy
salty	fishy	misty	static	rough
bitter	musty	dim	ring	prickly
spicy	minty	bright	buzz	sharp
rich	spicy	dark	sizzle	dull

2. Model writing a descriptive piece using as many sensory words as possible. For example:

   The Chocolate Brownie
   One of my favorite desserts is a chocolate brownie topped with icing and nuts. I love to smell the rich chocolate mixture as it bakes in the hot oven. I can hear the dark chocolate sizzling as it bakes. When the brownies are cooked and cooled, we spread sweet chocolate icing all over and sprinkle with pecans. The icing feels bumpy as it hardens. Then I get a taste of my sweet dessert.

3. As a follow-up, bring in several apples. Cut them in sections so that each child can touch, smell, taste, see, and hear details of the apples as they eat them. Ask students to write several describing sentences about their apples using appropriate sensory detail words—sparkle words!

Staying focused

EXPLANATION: Many students write stories with sentences that stray from the initial topic. Multiple mini-lessons are necessary to address this skill at different writing stages and with various writing modes. Demonstrations first should include obviously irrelevant sentences, then progress to increasingly more subtle off-topic examples.

SKILL FOCUS

Staying focused on the topic (narrative)

MATERIALS

Alexander and the Terrible, Horrible, No Good, Very Bad Day by Judith Viorst (optional)

QUICK HINTS

Have students write on self-selected topics. Allow a few minutes at the conclusion of their writing time for them to look over their papers and check that all of their sentences are on topic.

STEPS

1. Read aloud a brief story such as *Alexander and the Terrible, Horrible, No Good, Very Bad Day* by Judith Viorst. Ask students to listen for sentences that are not about the topic of the book. They will discover that all of the sentences belong. Explain why authors stay focused and only add sentences that belong in their stories.

2. Model writing a simple story with one or two sentences that don't belong, such as:

   The Squirrels and the Birdfeeder
   On Monday, Susan saw three frisky squirrels feeding under the birdfeeder. Susan had been watching a movie on television earlier. She saw one squirrel jump from the deck to the feeder. He had to hang upside down to reach the birdseed. Susan forgot to feed the cat. The squirrels ate all of the seed. Squirrels are fun to watch!

3. Ask students to decide which sentences do not belong in the story. Draw a line through them with a red marker.

4. Reread the story, omitting the sentences that stray from the topic. Agree that it's much better when all of the sentences stay on topic!

Expanding ideas

EXPLANATION: Beginning writers often write about a topic using sentences that are general in nature. Show students how to expand on an idea by adding more information.

SKILL FOCUS

Learning to elaborate on an idea for clarity and narrative richness

MATERIALS

6-inch balloon

QUICK HINTS

During individual writing conferences, tell students who are ready for this skill to mark three places in a piece of writing where ideas can be expanded. Use sticky notes or have them write these additional sentences on a strip of paper that can be taped, stapled, or glued where it should be inserted. This cut-and-paste technique helps young writers better understand revision.

STEPS

1. Model writing in generalities, such as in this paragraph:

   The Snowman

   Do you like to make a snowman? I think it is fun. The snow is cold and wet. It will stick together. I like to make a snowman.

2. Write the word *snowman* on a deflated balloon (a 6-inch balloon works best). Show the balloon to the class. Emphasize how small the word is. Blow air into the balloon and tell students that you are expanding the word. List on a chart words about a snowman as you slowly inflate the balloon at intervals. (Alternative idea: Write the words on the inflated balloon.) Your list might include:

white	*coat*
silly	*hat*
pack	*raisins*
rolls	*carrot*
icy	*twigs*

3. Add sentences using many of the words from the list to model how to expand on an idea. Reinforce the concept that you add sentences to your writing to make your idea more well-rounded with details, just as a balloon becomes well-rounded when filled up.

   The Snowman

   Do you like to make a snowman? I think it is fun. The snow is cold and wet. It will stick together. The icy snow packed into rolls will make three parts of the snowman. A hat and coat make him look silly. Raisins make the eyes and mouth. A carrot is the nose and twigs are the arms. I like to make a snowman.

Using a variety of words

EXPLANATION: Students need to recognize that overusing a word can make a piece of writing boring or otherwise detract from it. Words commonly overused by beginning writers include *very, said, good,* and *nice.* In this lesson, students learn to use synonyms to solve this problem, and in other lessons they learn to be more descriptive and precise.

SKILL FOCUS

Learning to vary word choice

MATERIALS

Colored transparency pens

QUICK HINTS

Design a ring of synonyms that can be used by students as they write. Write an overused word, such as *good* from the lesson on this page, in large letters on a colorful 3-by-5-inch notecard. Then write each synonym for that word on a separate white notecard. With a hole punch, place a hole in the upper left of each card. String on a silver ring clasp. Place in the writing center or hang where students have access. Encourage them to borrow the "synonym rings" as needed.

STEPS

1. On a transparency, write a short piece for your students that overuses a word, such as the following:

> *Saturday I went to see the Gamecocks play football. It was a good day for the game. We had a tailgate party before the game. The food was really good. We laughed and had a good time. We had good seats in the stadium where I could see everything. We had such a good time and our team won the game, too!*

2. Read the piece back with or to your students. Tell them that there's something you don't especially like about what you've written. There's a word that's used too often. Can students pick it out? Once the word *good* is identified as the overused word, highlight it with a colored pen.

3. Tell your students, "There are many words that mean the same thing as the word *good.* When we write, we try hard not to use certain words over and over. Our writing is better if we use lots of different words that have the same or nearly the same meaning. These words that mean the same thing are called synonyms."

4. With your students, brainstorm words that mean "good" but might be more descriptive. Your revised piece might look like this:

> *Saturday I went to see the Gamecocks play football. It*
> *was a ~~good~~ day for the game. We had a tailgate party*
>   *beautiful*
> *before the game. The food was really ~~good.~~ We laughed*
>   *scrumptious*
> *and had a ~~good~~ time. We had ~~good~~ seats in the stadium*
>   *great*   *perfect*
> *where I could see everything. We had such a good time*
> *and our team won the game, too!*

Understanding beginning, middle, and end

EXPLANATION: As beginning writers begin to elaborate by adding sentences to their narratives, they are ready to organize their writing into beginning, middle, and ending segments. Many states require this skill as a standard for writing in first grade.

SKILL FOCUS

Develop stories with a beginning, middle, and end

MATERIALS

- *Henry and Mudge Take the Big Test* by Cynthia Rylant
- Sticky notes (3 colors)

QUICK HINTS

Ask students to identify the beginning, middle, and end in stories they read. As you conference with students individually, reinforce their awareness level of this skill in books and in their writing.

STEPS

1. Read aloud *Henry and Mudge Take the Big Test* by Cynthia Rylant. This selection is an excellent example of a story in three distinct parts. Use three colors of sticky notes to mark the beginning, middle, and end of the story.

2. Model writing a brief narrative in which beginning, middle, and end are easily identified. For example:

   (the beginning) *Yesterday our class arrived at school ready for the field trip. The bus came at 9:00 a.m. and took us to the fire department.* (the middle) *We saw the new fire truck and the firefighter's coat, hat, and boots. We got to climb on the truck and pretended to be firefighters! The fire chief took our picture on the truck.* (the end) *We came back to school for lunch. Then we wrote about our exciting trip. We can't wait until the next field trip!*

3. Identify the three parts of the story with three different colors of sticky notes. Discuss how several sentences make up each section.

4. Ask students to write a story about a school event such as a field trip, a school carnival, a play, or a PTA program. Give each child three different colors of sticky notes to mark the beginning, middle, and end of their stories.

5. If necessary, extend the writing to the next day.

Sequencing, part one

EXPLANATION: Just as it's important for students to recognize sequential order in reading, it is equally important for them to think about sequencing in their writing. Students should understand, however, that sequential order is just one of many ways to organize writing. It is particularly important in narrative or story writing.

SKILL FOCUS

Using sequence in writing

MATERIALS

• Sentence strips
• A book showing sequential order (suggested: Lois Elhert's *Growing Vegetable Soup*)

QUICK HINTS

Find a good sample of student writing to show how that student put ideas in the right order. You might also take a student's writing and type each sentence onto a transparency (similar to the lesson here). Then let students come up to the overhead projector to arrange the sentences in the correct sequence.

STEPS

1. Choose a story to read to your students that has a clear and concise sequential order, such as Lois Elhert's *Growing Vegetable Soup*.

2. Prepare sentence strips with each main event of the story on a separate strip, such as:

   We planted the seed.

   We watered the ground each day.

   We weeded the garden.

   We picked the vegetables.

   We made the best soup ever!

3. Place the strips in scrambled order in a pocket chart. You might even laughingly pretend to drop the strips, "accidentally" scrambling them.

4. Ask students to help you arrange the strips in the right order. What happened first? What happened next? What happened last in the story?

5. After the class agrees on the order, reread the story to check your work. Tell the class you want to try something silly. Take the last event and move it to the top of the pocket chart. Read the events again. Ask the students if the story makes sense now. Is the order of the story important?

6. Remind students that when they write a story, they should think about the order. What should come first? What should come next? What should come last?

Sequencing, part two

EXPLANATION: Rather than using a published book as a springboard for exploring sequencing, this lesson uses an experience shared by the students and allows them to generate the sequential order themselves.

SKILL FOCUS

Sequential order

MATERIALS

- Art paper
- Crayons/markers

QUICK HINTS

See page 112 of the Appendix for another easy book for students to make emphasizing sequence.

STEPS

1. Choose a fun event that the class shared to create a class book with your students. The event may be a field trip you took, a play that you produced for parents, or a science experiment.

2. Remind students about the previous lesson, when you looked at how Lois Elhert's story was organized, one step at a time, in just the right order. Tell them that you're going to do that together with the event that you've chosen, and that they're going to make an accordion book!

3. First, compose the sequence of events on the overhead or on your chart. Then, after all of the events have been written, have students review the order.

4. Print each sentence on a separate piece of art paper. Number each page.

5. Ask students to illustrate the sentence on the same page. Students can work as partners or in small groups to plan, draw, and color.

6. When students have finished their illustrations, tape the pages together either end to end or side to side. Then fold the book accordion style.

7. Gather the students together to do a shared reading of their new book!

Telling about similarities and differences

EXPLANATION: Beginning writers are often asked to make comparisons when they are reading and when they are writing. Teach a writing mini-lesson following a similar mini-lesson on comparison as a reading strategy.

SKILL FOCUS

Comparing and contrasting

MATERIALS

- Chart paper
- *A Christmas Carol* by Charles Dickens
- *How the Grinch Stole Christmas* by Dr. Seuss

QUICK HINTS

Select books such as Kevin Henke's *Owen* and *Chrysanthemum*. Compare the problems in the two stories. See the chart below for an example of how to gather this information.

STEPS

1. Read from two books that have similarities and differences, such as *A Christmas Carol* and *How the Grinch Stole Christmas*.

2. Select two characters to compare and contrast, such as Scrooge and the Grinch.

3. Prepare a Venn diagram organizing how the characters are alike and different. For example:

Scrooge

took money

had a job

would not celebrate Christmas

ghosts changed him

mean

did not know how to love

took from others

lonely

The Grinch

took toys

didn't have a job

tried to stop Christmas from coming

The Whos changed him

4. Ask students to write several sentences about how the two characters were alike and different. For example:
   Scrooge and the Grinch took from others. Scrooge and the Grinch were lonely. The Whos changed the Grinch, but ghosts changed Scrooge.

Owen	Chrysanthemum	Both
Wanted to take his baby blanket to school, but his mom would not let him.	Students at school made fun of her name and she wanted to change it.	Both problems were solved and the stories had a happy ending.
His mom solved the problem.	Her teacher solved the problem.	

Using concrete examples (similes)

EXPLANATION: A mini-lesson for beginning writers on concrete examples explores what they will later learn to call "similes." Helping young writers to make their writing clear is the focus of this lesson.

SKILL FOCUS

Using concrete images to clarify

QUICK HINTS

Each time a concrete example is used in students' writing, let them draw a dollar sign over it. Then ask "How much is your story worth?" and see who has the most expensive story.

List on a chart several of the ways to make writing better, such as:
- Using sensory words
- Using concrete examples
- Combining sentences
- Painting a picture with describing words

STEPS

1. List several adjectives and verbs and a concrete example of each. For example:
   - cold—as cold as ice
   - hot—as hot as fire
   - soft—as soft as fur
   - close—as close as the nose on your face
   - high—as high as a kite

2. Model using concrete examples to make your writing clearer. First, write the paragraph below without the concrete examples (in parentheses). Discuss how difficult it is to see what is described. Then add the concrete examples and read again to discover how much clearer the writing has become.

   My Circus Trip

   My trip to the circus was full of surprises. First, we were able to get seats in the front row. The clowns were (as) close (as the nose on my face). I laughed so hard (that I almost cried). Next, the lions were not in their cages. The tamer had one on a leash (so) near me (that I could hear his soft purring). Then my name was called to ride the elephant. My heart was beating (as fast as a drummer beats his drum). The surprises were fun, and I had a great time!

3. Over the next few weeks, continue reminding students to make their writing clear by using concrete examples.

Paragraphs with a central idea and related details

EXPLANATION: Students need to learn to support their ideas with examples or facts. Graphic organizers such as the one used in this lesson offer some structure that students may find handy for organization.

SKILL FOCUS

Writing paragraphs with a central idea and related ideas or details

QUICK HINTS

As pre-writing for informational pieces, give students the table graphic organizer (see Steps) in separate pieces of construction paper. Have them write a topic sentence and a question. Then have them write information on each of the legs that answers the question, such as:

Spiders have a strange way of eating. How do I know that?

They turn food into liquid.	They usually eat only insects.	They trap prey in a web.	They poison with a bite.

STEPS

1. Start a piece of writing by making a simple statement, such as "My cat wants to be a person." Follow the statement with the question, "How do I know this?" Use this as a cue that, when writing about this statement, several reasons should be given to show that it is true. For example:

   My Cat Wants to Be a Person!

   My cat, Circie, wants to be a person just like you and me! How do I know this? Every morning as I get ready for school, she sits at the sink and watches me carefully. I think she wants to figure out how to put on make-up! When I get my breakfast, she runs to her bowl to eat just like me. When I get dressed, she sits on my clothes. I think she wants to wear them! So, you can see now that my cat wants to be a person!

2. After you've written your piece, tell students, "Boys and girls, I want to show you something about my writing today. This piece of writing reminds me of a table! Isn't that strange? Let me show you what I mean." Then begin to sketch a table such as the one below and add, "On the table top, I'm going to put what my piece is about and the question I want to answer about it."

My cat wants to be a person. How do I know this?

3. "Now I'm going to draw the legs of the table that hold it up." Sketch:

Watches me put on make-up.	Eats when I eat.	Sits on my clothes.	

4. Tell students, "When you write, think about supporting your ideas like legs support a table."

Characters for narratives

EXPLANATION: Students often get stuck in their writing because they cannot think of anyone to write about. Beginning writers' lives revolve around themselves, family, and friends. These groups of people are natural resources for characters for their narratives.

SKILL FOCUS

Choosing characters

MATERIALS

8½-by-11-inch drawing paper

QUICK HINTS

Later in the year, beginning writers are more likely to be able to use their imaginations to make up characters for their stories. Reading aloud many imaginative narratives encourages this mode of writing.

STEPS

1. Fold a paper in half hot-dog style (the long way). Write "family" at the top of one column made by the fold and "friends" at the top of the other. Explain that the characters in our stories can come from our real lives.

2. Model writing names of your family and friends. For example:

Family	*Friends*
husband Don	*Docia*
daughter Melissa	*Joe*
daughter Susan	*Linda*
brother Sonny	*Sam*
sister-in-law Linda	*Tamah*

3. Set a timer for a few minutes to allow students to talk about family and friends with a partner.

4. Tell students to write names of family and friends on their own folded papers. This paper can remain in their writing folders for future reference.

5. As a follow-up on another day, have students develop a jot list of memories that involve their family and friends. For example:

    a special birthday
    a trip to the zoo
    a school play
    a snowball fight
    a ride on a boat
    going to camp

6. To write a narrative, have students choose character names from each column and a memory from their jot list.

Settings for narratives

EXPLANATION: As students hear about the many settings of stories read aloud to them, they build a reservoir of places and times to write about. In this lesson, students brainstorm lists of settings from their own lives that they can use in their stories.

— SKILL FOCUS —

Choosing settings for narratives

— QUICK HINTS —

Use the brainstorming lists from this lesson to create aids for your class writing center. Write settings and characters on note cards—one per card. Use them in this way:

- Allow all students the opportunity to sort the cards into the two groups—settings and characters—so that they see the variety of options with the categories.
- After students have sorted the cards, punch a hole in the top left corner of each card. Bind all settings on one ring and all characters on another ring. Make the rings available in the writing center for students to get ideas for their writing.

STEPS

1. Ask your students to fold a paper in half hot-dog style (the long way). Have them write *places* at the top of one column and *times* at the top of the other.

2. Model writing places and periods of time that might be used in your narratives.

Places	*Times*
home	*one second*
school	*one minute*
playground	*one hour*
church	*one day*
classroom	*one week*
cafeteria	*one month*
shopping center	*one year*
sports event	*spring*
restaurant	*summer*
state fair	*fall*
	winter
	Christmas
	Valentine's Day

3. Ask students to write places and times on their folded papers. This paper can remain in their writing folders for future reference.

Multiple-day writing, part one

EXPLANATION: Beginning writers often have trouble sustaining their work on one piece of writing over several days. A great deal of modeling by the teacher might be necessary before students feel comfortable reconnecting to a previous piece of writing.

SKILL FOCUS

Sustaining interest in a piece of writing

QUICK HINTS

It is very helpful to store your daily writing samples so that you can go back occasionally to revise or edit them. Also, you might keep them for next year to remind yourself of how you taught certain writing skills. An expandable folder makes a good storage file and allows you to label the dividers according to the type of lesson for easy retrieval.

STEPS

1. Students dearly love the stories you share about when you were little! Begin your lesson by modelling a topic map of things you could write about from when you were their age. For example:

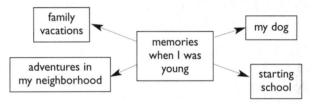

2. Think aloud about which topic appeals to you the most. After selecting one, put some branches on that portion of the topic map to plan the details of what you'll write, such as:

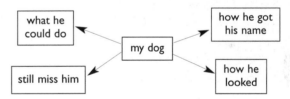

3. Use your map to begin writing the first paragraph. For example:

My Dog
When I was seven years old, I had a dog named Caruso. He was named after a famous singer because he was big like the singer and he had a deep, deep bark. Caruso was an English Shepherd. His fur was soft and fluffy, and he was black with white spots.

4. Keep the length of the passage appropriate to the attention span of your students. Do a brief edit and then remark to your students that there's still more that you want to tell about your dog so you'll continue this tomorrow.

Multiple-day writing, part two

EXPLANATION: Teachers must dispense with daily prompts in order to encourage students to write on a topic for as long as it takes to say what needs to be said. Some students might finish within one Writing Workshop, while others might attempt to write "the great American novel." Model for them how to extend their writing, but accept that some may not be ready for that step.

SKILL FOCUS

Sustaining interest in a piece of writing

QUICK HINTS

Ask some students to share their writing at the conclusion of the Writing Workshop time. Tell them that you'd like their peers to listen carefully to what they share, and to ask any questions about what else they'd like to know about the topic. On sticky notes, make notes about questions asked and give them to the students who shared so that they might write more on a subsequent day.

STEPS

1. Tell students that instead of starting a new piece, you'd like to continue telling about your dog, Caruso. To get started again, read your first day's piece aloud to help reconnect to your earlier thoughts. Then review your topic map from part one to check the ideas you've covered and the ideas you still might add. Tell students, "There are so many more things I want you to know about Caruso. So far, I've really only told you how he got his name and how he looked. I want to tell you some of the funny things he did, too! That's what I'll write about next." Then write:

   Caruso thought he was a person. He loved to greet the mailman each day. He loved to sleep in the bed with me. He loved to eat any leftover food that I could share with him. He also learned to open and close some of the doors in our house. He was so smart and lovable! Many years later, I still miss him!

2. Do a quick check of your work at the end of your writing and remark that you're glad you can keep working on pieces that you want to add to. Invite the kids to look through some of the pieces they've already written and ask themselves this question: "Are there more ideas that I can add to make my writing more interesting?"

Section Five: Writing for Real Purposes and Audiences

The power of written communication is all around us, and as adults it's easy to appreciate writing's power. We see it in letters from friends, newspaper articles, advertisements, and other printed materials. We notice how a well-turned phrase can sometimes diffuse a difficult situation, persuade us to take action, evoke a range of emotions from laughter to tears, or inform us of issues we need to know about.

Students send notes and letters they've written to real people through the school's mail system.

Beginning writers need the benefits of reading—and writing—for authentic purposes as much as adults do. If students' exposure to writing is mostly just addressing prompts assigned by the teacher, or if it primarily entails writing in a journal that only the student and the teacher will see, then they will have great difficulty making the connection between writing and the real world. Students need to see that their writing can affect change and elicit responses, can make people laugh or think about things in a different way, and can teach their peers about things they didn't know. Only then can they take ownership of their writing—and they might even embrace the laborious process of making their writing the best it can be!

What are some purposes and audiences for beginning writers? There are so many reasons to write—and so little time! Students may want to write a letter to a sick classmate or to the cafeteria lady who has done something special for them. They may write a poem that they recite to their classmates' delight. They will likely construct dozens of books over the course of the year to entertain their family and friends. Some teachers even give students the opportunity to dedicate the books they make, which certainly creates an audience for writing! Students might also

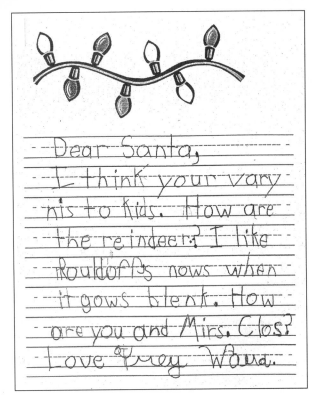

Students write best about the things that matter most to them.

design a class or school newsletter that keeps parents, students, and other teachers abreast of what's happening in the classroom. The list of purposes and audiences is limitless!

Just think how truly sad it would be if your students felt that the only reason for writing was to pass a test or to fill a journal to earn an occasional smiley face! We want them to know the personal fulfillment that writing can bring, and also to know the power of the written word far beyond the classroom in real-life contexts. The lessons in this section help you share this fulfillment and understanding with your students.

Generating questions for interviews

EXPLANATION: Children are filled with curiosity, so asking questions is their specialty! Teach students to satisfy their curiosity through reading and writing.

SKILL FOCUS

Posing effective questions for informational writing

RESOURCES

Contact a person in your school or community, such as the principal, a career professional, or a football player and set up a classroom visit.

QUICK HINTS

For a quick and easy bulletin board, cover a space on a wall with butcher paper. Write at the top: "Things We Wonder." Invite students to write any of the questions they have about classroom studies on this board. Remember to add things you wonder as well. These questions can become good topics for research or informational writing in the future.

STEPS

1. Announce to students that a special person will be visiting the class soon. (For this lesson, the visitor is a veterinarian; the visitor for your class can be anyone you choose.) Let students know that the visit will allow them to learn a lot about veterinarians.

2. To be prepared for the visit, have the class make a list of questions—things that everyone wants to know about a veterinarian's job. Be prepared to stimulate students' thinking if they hesitate. Questions might include:

   How did you get ready to be a veterinarian?
   How long did you have to go to school?
   Why did you want to be a veterinarian?
   What's the biggest animal you've cared for?
   What's the smallest animal you've cared for?
   How can we keep our pets healthy?
   Do animals get the same illnesses that we do?
   How is taking care of an animal different from taking care of a person?

3. Write down the questions on a chart. You may want to record the student's name after the question he/she has asked. As the questions are written, remind students about the kind of punctuation mark necessary at the end of questions, and how these sentences are different from "telling" sentences.

4. Practice reading the sentences with your students several times before the day of the visit from your special person.

5. Have the chart of questions on hand during the interview and let the students ask the questions.

Friendly letters

EXPLANATION: Students need to know that there are many real-life purposes for writing. Writing a friendly letter is one of these, and it represents one of the first audiences that students learn to address.

SKILL FOCUS

Using an appropriate format for writing a friendly letter

QUICK HINTS

Replicating a postal service in your class and/or school gives students a real purpose for writing. Let them learn about responsibility as they become mail carriers or letter sorters.

March 20

Dear Trent,

   We miss you since you moved away. We have been very busy. We took a trip to the fire station and got to sit on the fire truck! Our gerbil, Squeaky, had babies, and they are really cute. Also, we've been growing beans for science. We are all reading a lot now, too!
   How is your new school? Please write and let us know!
                    Love,
                    The Class

STEPS

1. Share with your students, "I've been writing letters to you this year in our Morning Message. I usually share with you interesting things that we'll be doing each day. I'll bet that you've seen your moms and dads write letters at home to mail to friends, telling them interesting things about what they've been doing lately and asking what their friends have been doing. We call these 'friendly letters,' which seems to be just the right name for them!"

2. If appropriate, choose a student who has moved away to write to: "Boys and girls, Trent left our class two weeks ago to move with his family to another state. I have his address, and I think he would love to hear from us. Let's write a friendly letter to him together!"

3. Sketch a template to show students how to organize the paper for a friendly letter with these parts:

4. Let students brainstorm about what they think their friend might want to hear about, such as their field trip to the fire station or a favorite book the class has read lately.

   ```
   Date

   Greeting,

   Body (What we
   want to say)--------
   -----------------------
   -----------------------

                  Closing,
                  Signature
   ```

5. Write the letter, using students' ideas to guide you.

6. Tell students that they should let the person they're writing to know that they're interested in what he or she is doing, too. Ask some questions that the person can answer when he or she writes back. (See sample letter at left.)

Invitations

EXPLANATION: Writing an invitation is a good skill for students to learn—and it's authentic writing, of course. The class might invite parents to an open house, to the PTA meeting, or to a special school event.

—(SKILL FOCUS)—

Using an appropriate format to write an invitation

—(MATERIALS)—

- Construction paper
- Crayons
- Markers

—(QUICK HINTS)—

Ask students to write invitations requesting their buddy readers (from the upper grades) come to visit their classroom.

STEPS

1. Tell students that the school Spring Fling (or other school event) will take place soon. The principal has asked the class to write an invitation to include in the next school newsletter, to be posted on the bulletin board outside the school office, or to be displayed in some other way. To plan the invitation, ask students to help you think of important information to include.

2. Make a jot list of information about the event, including:
   Date, time, and place
   Types of food
   Activities

3. After brainstorming the above, write the invitation.

> ### Come One! Come All!
> to the
> Spring Fling
> on
> Saturday, May 15, 2004
> 10:00 a.m. – 2:00 p.m.
> Wood Elementary School
>
> Enjoy hot dogs, cookies, pies, and cakes!
> Play games! Get your face painted!
>
> See you there!

Thank-you notes

EXPLANATION: Many opportunities throughout the year give students the chance to write authentic thank-you notes. For example, if the school PTA gives a book to the classroom on the teacher's birthday, the class can write thank-you notes to the PTA president. Students practice their writing skills and good etiquette at the same time!

SKILL FOCUS

Writing a thank-you note

MATERIALS

Paper for stationery

QUICK HINTS

Provide students with real stationery. It is also motivating for students to illustrate their notes. Include new writing paper and pencils in the writing center to encourage note writing.

STEPS

1. This activity should be made as authentic as possible so that there is a real audience to receive students' thank-you notes.

2. Share with students that you received a new book for the class from the PTA on your birthday, and that it is always proper to write a thank-you note after receiving a gift.

3. Demonstrate the template:

4. Plan the body of the note, including an opening sentence, three or four sentences expressing gratitude and examples of how the gift will be used, and a closing sentence.

```
                              Date

Greeting,

Body (What we
want to say)--------
------------------------
------------------------

                          Closing,
                          Signature
```

5. Then write on an overhead or chart:

> *May 14, 2004*
>
> *Dear Mr. Johnson,*
>
> *Our class would like to thank you for our teacher's birthday gift. The book is one of our favorites. Mrs. Lyles read it aloud to us yesterday. We can't wait to get to read it on our own. The book will have a special place on our bookshelf. Please stop by our room and listen to us read.*
>
> *Thank you,*
> *Mrs. Lyles's Class*

6. After writing this class note, brainstorm other reasons for thank-you notes and ask the class to write individual notes for authentic purposes.

Writing poems that rhyme

EXPLANATION: Students need to know that not all poems must rhyme; however, primary students really do enjoy experimenting with rhyming poetry. They love the sound of rhymes, and they need the phonemic practice that rhymes offer. They also need to hear lots of rhyming poetry read aloud to understand the concept before attempting to write their own.

SKILL FOCUS

Understanding rhyme through poetry writing

RESOURCES

Recommended poetry books include:
- *in the swim* by Douglas Florian
- *Best Friends* by Lee Bennett Hopkins
- *A Hippopotamusn't and Other Animal Poems* by J. Patrick Lewis
- *A Lucky Thing* by Alice Schertle

QUICK HINTS

Put students in groups of two to four to write interactive poems. If you've been studying word families, assign each group a different one, such as *-ain, -and, -ook, -ig,* and *-op*, on which to base their poem. Bind poems together to make a class book—and to reinforce phonemic awareness.

STEPS

1. Tell students that you're going to show them a fun, easy way to write poems that rhyme. Start the lesson by choosing a topic word and then brainstorming other words that sound like it. (They don't have to have the same spelling patterns.) Perhaps the class just read about a bear, and so wants to write a poem about one. List words that sound like *bear*:

bear	*hair*	*stare*	*rare*	*fair*	*care*
dare	*fare*	*pear*	*tear*	*wear*	*flare*

2. The rhyme for this model poem will occur at the end of each line, which is the easiest rhyme scheme to attempt. Tell your students that you're in the mood for a silly poem. Start your poem with a good first line that ends with one of the word family words, such as:

   I saw a bear
   When I went to the fair
   He had no hair
   Which was very rare
   But I didn't stare!

3. You might want to point out that there are four spelling patterns that all sound alike in this poem!

4. Next, try brainstorming rhymes for another word with your students. Let them help you write a poem using some of the words as ending rhymes. Remind them that poems can be funny, silly, serious, happy, or sad. Tell them, "It's so much easier to write when you decide what mood you want your poem to express before you get started."

5. If writing the interactive poem works well, ask students to try writing a poem on their own.

Shape poems

EXPLANATION: Poetry can be great fun for students of all ages! First graders particularly enjoy experimenting with shape poetry. It causes them to think about good word choices and also allows them to play with shapes that relate to their words and ideas. Shape poetry also provides an opportunity to teach students that poems don't have to rhyme.

SKILL FOCUS

Writing concrete poems

MATERIALS

- Shape poems such as those in *Doodle Dandies: Poems that Take Shape* by J. Patrick Lewis
- Shape patterns; tracing pencils; paper in various colors

QUICK HINTS

Using a die-cut machine, cut lots of different shapes from construction paper. Make some of them single-layered and some double-layered and hinged like a book. Make hinged books by moving the fold to the inside of the edge where the blade will cut. Students will love writing poetry in and around these!

fold →

poem on inside

My Pumpkin Poem

STEPS

1. Find some good examples of poems to read and explore with your students to give them a "feel" for what a poem sounds like. Choose examples of poems that rhyme and some that don't rhyme.

2. Tell your students that you want to show them a creative way to write poetry in shapes. Choose a shape from your collection of die-cuts. For example, choose a cat shape and trace the outline onto your transparency.

3. Along the outside or inside of the outline, write words that describe the object, using descriptive words and some expressive verbs. Here's an attempt at a cat-shaped poem:

   Crawling and creeping; lazily sleeping; curiously peeping; sipping and eating— my loving cat!

4. Let students choose a shape pattern or invite them to draw shapes of anything they might want to describe using a few descriptive words. Remind them that these poems should be brief and usually aren't in complete sentences. Students should use strong describing words and action verbs.

5. These poems will certainly make a great display outside or inside your classroom!

Narrative writing

EXPLANATION: Later in the year, young writers may begin to branch out from writing personal narratives to writing made-up stories. Daily read-alouds from many different genres begin to influence them. Mystery and fantasy genres may be represented in their writing. This mini-lesson on the characteristics of narrative writing assists them in organizing their ideas.

SKILL FOCUS

Knowing the characteristics of narrative writing

RESOURCES

Books representing different types of narratives, such as:

- *Amazing Grace* by Mary Hoffman
- *Bear's Dream* by Janet Slingsby
- *The Mystery of the Missing Dog* by Elizabeth Levy
- *Possum Magic* by Mem Fox

QUICK HINTS

Give students three colors of sticky notes. Mark one with a "b" for beginning, one with an "m" for middle, and one with an "e" for end. Tell them to mark one of their narratives with the sticky notes to indicate the beginning, middle, and end.

STEPS

1. Discuss different types of narratives, such as personal, story, mystery, and fantasy. Share familiar books that fit each category (see Resources at left for authors).

   Personal: *Amazing Grace*
   Story: *Bear's Dream*
   Mystery: *The Mystery of the Missing Dog*
   Fantasy: *Possum Magic*

2. Discuss the characteristics that are common to a narrative.

- Beginning. This part of the story usually introduces the character(s) and the setting (place and time), although these elements may change throughout the story.
- Middle. The events unfold in this part as the writer develops the plot. There is usually a sequence that allows the reader to make predictions.
- End. The story draws to a conclusion. The ending may be predictable or a surprise, but usually there is a resolution.

3. Add the narrative characteristics to a chart on a transparency (below) as you discuss each one. Begin to fill in the chart with brief summaries of these characteristics as you read narratives aloud. Students will have fun comparing the different beginnings and endings used by different authors.

Book Title	Beginning	Middle	End

4. Invite students to write a narrative with a beginning, middle, and end.

5. During individual conferences, ask students questions about their stories and emphasize narrative characteristics.

Descriptive writing

EXPLANATION: Young writers need to explore lots of different types of reading and writing. As they explore a variety of print, they begin to understand that different types of writing serve different purposes. With ample exposure, they'll soon begin to identify the kinds of writing by their distinctive characteristics.

SKILL FOCUS

Knowing the characteristics of descriptive writing

QUICK HINTS

When you review a piece of writing with students to note the sensory words and phrases, you might draw a corresponding symbol right on the lines where those words appear. For example:

 eye = sight

 finger = touch

 tongue = taste

 ear = hear

 nose = smell

STEPS

1. Model a descriptive piece of writing so that students will be able to discuss with you the characteristics of this writing. A hook for getting their attention might be, "Boys and girls, today I want you to feel my writing!" Your writing might be as follows:

   Winter Is Here!

   Yesterday I went for a walk in my neighborhood. The <u>wind was howling</u> through <u>the bare branches</u> of the trees, and my <u>ears and nose were cold</u>. The day was <u>cloudy and grey</u>. Each step I took had a <u>crunch or a pop</u> to it because I stepped on <u>brittle leaves and acorns</u>. I could <u>smell wood burning</u> in my neighbors' fireplaces and even some good <u>wintertime foods</u> cooking. From the <u>smell of cinnamon</u>, I'm sure Mrs. Gardner was baking an <u>apple pie</u>! I could tell on my walk that winter is certainly in the air!

2. Do a Quick Check of your writing for basic errors after you've finished writing. (Sometimes, of course, we make mistakes to model how students will handle them.)

3. Ask students to assist you in underlining things in your paragraph that help them to see, feel, taste, hear, or smell what you've written. (See the underlining above.)

4. Write the words *describe* and *descriptive* for your students. Explain that sometimes we write to describe so that people can use their senses of sight, touch, taste, hearing, and smell to enjoy our writing. Ask them how their writing "feels"!

5. Brainstorm with students the types of topics they might write about in the future that would allow them to describe (seasons, animals, friends, pictures, flowers, dinosaurs, etc.).

Informational writing

EXPLANATION: Students love reading nonfiction; in this lesson, students explore various kinds of informational texts as a springboard to their own nonfiction writing.

SKILL FOCUS

Knowing the characteristics of informational writing

MATERIALS

- Magazines
- Memos
- Nonfiction books
- Newspapers

QUICK HINTS

Start an "Experts" bulletin board. As students share things that are unique, add their names to the board with their topic alongside it. When everyone is listed as an expert, you might have them interview each other about these topics.

STEPS

1. With students seated in cooperative groups, furnish each group with a different type of informational writing. For example, put copies of *Scholastic News* at one table, *Ranger Rick* magazines at another table, and nonfiction books about sharks, trucks, countries, and spiders on another table. Perhaps even put newspapers at another table.

2. Ask students in each group to study the materials for two minutes and to record what the group thinks is the main reason why someone would read the material.

3. After two minutes, have the groups rotate their materials to another group and repeat the process. Continue rotating the materials as time allows (each group doesn't necessarily have to review all of the materials).

4. Ask groups to report what they recorded. Write their responses on the board or on a transparency. Responses will likely include: to learn something, to find out the news, to know more about the topic, and so on.

5. Write the words *informational text* for the students to see. Ask if they can find the little word hiding in the big word. Underline the word part *inform* as students discover it.

6. Let students know that they will be writing informational pieces this year to teach others what they know. Brainstorm with students the types of topics they might write about in the future that would allow them to inform. Let them know that they are all experts on different subjects. Your list could include topics like: How Corn Grows, Sharks, Sea Animals, How Caterpillars Change into Moths, How to Wash a Dog, Making Cookies, The First Thanksgiving, Caring for a Gerbil, Being a Good Batter

Informational writing (science)

EXPLANATION: By integrating grade-level Science content into the writing block, teachers can streamline their instructional day. For this reason—and because students are naturally curious about science-related topics—this lesson uses Science to integrate reading, writing, and content.

SKILL FOCUS

Writing informational text (Science)

MATERIALS & RESOURCES

- *The Important Book* by Margaret Wise Brown
- The Important Poem frame (see page 121)
- Science textbook
- *One Bean* by Anne Rockwell and Megan Halsey

QUICK HINTS

"When students connect the study of grammar and language patterns to the wider purposes of communication and artistic development, they are considerably more likely to incorporate such knowledge into their working knowledge."

—*Standards for the English Language Arts* (NCTE and IRA, p. 37), 1996

STEPS

1. Read aloud *The Important Book* by Margaret Wise Brown. Review the structure of this type of writing. (The first and last sentences are the same.) Read aloud *One Bean* for additional background information and excellent illustrations about plants.

2. Review the Science textbook chapter about plants. Identify important details. Help students determine the most important thing about plants to use for the first and last sentence in their writing. For example: "The important thing about plants is that they have the same needs and parts."

3. For a focused writing assignment, have students write an Important Poem about plants. They may use the Important Poem frame to add several details about plants (see Appendix, page 121). Here's an example of an Important Poem about plants:

    The important thing about plants is that they have the same needs and parts.

    They need air, water, and sunlight to grow.
    They have roots, stems, and leaves.
    They have roots to hold them in place.
    Roots take in water and nutrients from the soil.
    Stems hold the plant up, support the leaves, and carry the food supply.
    Leaves take in energy from the sun.

    But the most important thing about plants is that they have the same needs and parts.

Informational writing (social studies)

EXPLANATION: Social Studies topics provide an excellent opportunity for integrating writing and content, as well as for reading and writing nonfiction.

SKILL FOCUS

Writing informational text (Social Studies)

MATERIALS & RESOURCES

- *The Important Book* by Margaret Wise Brown
- *One Hundred Is a Family* by Pam Munoz Ryan
- The Important Poem frame (see page 121)

QUICK HINTS

Use the text of *The Important Book* as a quick assessment of what students know about content in Social Studies.

STEPS

1. Read aloud two or three poems from *The Important Book* by Margaret Wise Brown. Discuss the pattern of this type of poem: the first and last sentences are the same, with details in the middle.

2. Tell students that the class will write an Important Poem about families. Build background by reading aloud *One Hundred Is a Family* by Pam Munoz Ryan.

3. Lead a discussion about the characteristics of families that make them important to us. Discuss the basic needs met by our families. Slot these ideas into a web graphic organizer as shown:

4. Guide students in choosing the most important thing about families for the first and last sentence. For example: "The important thing about our families is that they love us." Write this sentence in the transparency of the poetry frame.

5. Ask students to copy the first and last sentence from the transparency onto their papers. Next, have them add important things about their own families on lines 2, 3, and 4.

6. Invite students to share their poems with the class and add them to a class book called "The Important Things About Our Families."

Writing to respond

EXPLANATION: As students begin to read more involved texts in guided reading, they are expected to be able to formulate responses to questions asked about those texts. Many state reading tests require that answers to questions about reading passages be answered in complete sentences. In this lesson, students gain experience in writing to answer a question or prompt.

SKILL FOCUS

Writing to respond to a question

RESOURCE

Our Living Forests by Allan Fowler

QUICK HINTS

Model composing responses to questions many times before asking your students to try this type of writing independently.

STEPS

1. On a transparency, provide a copy of a passage from students' guided reading. Prepare three questions about it. The answers to two of the questions should be "right there," so that students just have to find them. One question should require making an inference, so that students have to "figure out" the answer. This mini-lesson focuses on how to construct a response to this last question. An example you might use is:

    Our Living Forests
    There are many beautiful forest areas all over the world. The kinds of trees you find in each forest depend on the weather and soil there. Evergreen forests grow in places that are usually cool. Evergreens have needles instead of leaves and are never bare. As they shed their needles, new ones grow. This is why they are called evergreens.

    1. *Where do evergreen forests grow?* (The answer can be found in the text: Evergreens grow in cool places.)
    2. *What do evergreens have instead of leaves?* (The answer can be found in the text: Evergreens have needles instead of leaves.)
    3. *Why would evergreen forests not grow well in very hot and dry climates?* (The answer cannot be found; it must be figured out.)

2. Discuss with students how to answer this last type of question. First, look for clues. Words such as *weather, soil,* and *cool* are important. Use a marker to highlight these words and important sentences. In order to never be bare, the trees must have lots of water. An appropriate answer might be: *Evergreens need cool climates and lots of water to grow.*

Tell me a story

EXPLANATION: Once beginning writers have been exposed to stories through read-alouds, story writing can be modeled. Story writing should be one of the focused writing topics students experience. This lesson on writing stories should be an extension of the lesson on characteristics of narrative writing on page 85.

SKILL FOCUS

Writing stories

MATERIALS

Chart of characteristics of narrative writing from a previous lesson (page 85)

QUICK HINTS

An engaging homework assignment is to have parents brainstorm about and list with their child family events and stories from when the child was younger. Add these lists to students' writing folders.

Have students trace the outline of their hand on a piece of paper. On the palm, ask them to write "Good, Bad, and Sad Stories." Have them write one topic for a story on each finger.

STEPS

1. Tell the class that you have an interesting story to share. Talk about the characteristics of a story that the class charted from a previous lesson. (See page 85 and refer to the chart if you made one.)

2. Talk about the beginning of stories and how the character(s) and setting are introduced. Then write:
   Peepers, the Sugar Glider
   It all began when Peepers got out of her cage. It was late at night.

3. Next, discuss how events unfold through the middle of the story. Then continue to add to the middle:
   The bedroom door was closed. Peepers squeezed her tiny, furry body under the door. She scampered down the stairs. She climbed up and down the Christmas tree, knocking ornaments to the floor. Bows flew off of packages! The critter ran behind the TV and scaled the rock fireplace. We were not sure we could catch her.

4. Discuss how stories come to a conclusion at the end. Then continue writing by adding an ending.
   Maybe Peepers was getting tired, because she began to slow down. We grabbed a towel and scooped her up! Back to her cage she went with fun memories of her escape.

5. Ask students to choose a story topic and write several sentences that convey a beginning, middle, and end.

Story patterns

EXPLANATION: Many children's books are written in patterns that provide reading support. These favorite books are often in big book form and can be read and reread by groups and individuals. Class books and little books can be written with similar patterns in mind.

SKILL FOCUS

Borrowing ideas from favorite authors (story patterns)

RESOURCES

- *If You Give a Mouse a Cookie* by Laura Numeroff
- *If You Give a Moose a Muffin* by Laura Numeroff

QUICK HINTS

Remind your students of different types of patterned books. Some have recurring words. Some are ABC books. Others are written as letters or postcards. Help students identify unique patterns as these types of books are read aloud.

STEPS

1. Laura Numeroff writes many children's books that are circular stories. The stories end back at the beginning. Favorites are *If You Give a Mouse a Cookie* and *If You Give a Moose a Muffin.* Read these books and others to your students. Discuss the similar patterns in each book.

2. With the class, compose a circular story using Numeroff's books as the pattern. For example:

    If You Give a Cricket a Cake

    If you give a cricket a cake,
    He'll want some ice cream to go with it.
    He'll probably have a full tummy,
    So he'll want to take a nap.
    He'll ask you for a pillow.
    When you give him the pillow,
    He'll probably ask for a blanket.
    When you give him the blanket,
    He'll go to sleep and dream.
    When he wakes up, he will probably
    Ask for something to eat.
    If you give him ice cream,
    He'll want cake to go with it.

3. Ask students to work on writing a story that ends back at the beginning.

Text structure

EXPLANATION: Many state curricula require primary students to write pieces with various text structures. The most common of these are story, informational, and poetry. If students read from a variety of text structures, they develop the ability to write in different text structures. They must read or have read to them many examples before they feel comfortable using different text structures in their own writing.

SKILL FOCUS

Borrowing ideas from favorite authors (text structure)

MATERIALS & RESOURCES

• Informational books by Gail Gibbons (optional)
• Markers

QUICK HINTS

Science is possibly the most motivating content for reading and writing. Use science content to fully engage your students.

Coach students during individual writing conference time. Help them grow in their ability to write facts about a topic on which they are an expert.

STEPS

1. Read aloud many examples of informational text by Gail Gibbons or other authors. (Gail Gibbons is an outstanding author of informational text for the primary grades. Many primary teachers use her books for reading lessons.)

2. Show students how the sentences tell facts about the pictures. Explain to them that the facts follow a logical order and that the reader has to use the information to draw conclusions about the topic.

3. Model writing a simple informational piece that is similar to the structure used by Gail Gibbons or other authors. For example:

The Seasons
Would you like to know about the seasons? The four seasons are winter, spring, summer, and fall. Each season lasts for three months. Sometimes the weather changes when the season changes. It is fun to learn about the seasons.

4. Ask students to identify the facts. Have them come to the overhead and underline each fact with a different color marker.

5. Ask students to write on focused topics from previous science units. Using previously-studied content provides the background knowledge needed to write informational text. Some possible topics include: weather, animals, plants, and the five senses.

Sentence variety

EXPLANATION: We teach mini-lessons to help students improve their short, choppy sentences by combining sentences (see page 62). Later, it becomes important to teach about sentence variety, including different lengths and types of sentences. This lesson uses picture books to help students develop the skills to write a variety of sentences.

SKILL FOCUS

Borrowing ideas from favorite authors (sentence variety)

RESOURCE

Chameleons Are Cool by Martin Jenkins

QUICK HINTS

Some beginning writers need more help than others with identifying sentence variety. Use individual conference time to assist these students.

STEPS

1. Read aloud good books that use many different types and lengths of sentences. *Chameleons Are Cool* by Martin Jenkins is a fun informational book that is an excellent choice.

2. After reading this book for pleasure, ask students to examine with you sentences in the book. Find examples of long and short sentences. Look for statements, questions, and exclamatory sentences.

3. Write an example of each of the above on a chart (see below). Lead students to understand how using a variety of sentences makes their writing more interesting.

Chameleons Are Cool

• Long Sentence	"So if two chameleons bump into each other, things can get pretty lively."
• Short Sentence	"They are grumpy."
• Statement	"Chameleons feed on all sorts of creepy crawlies."
• Question	"How could you possibly resist a pocket-sized, bad-tempered, color-changing, swivel-eyed, snail-paced, long-tongued sharp shooter?"
• Exclamatory Sentence	"If chameleons aren't cool, then I don't know what is!"

4. Ask students to look at a draft of their own writing. Have them look for long and short sentences and sentences of different types. Work with them on revising their writing so that it has a variety of sentences.

Ideas

EXPLANATION: As the last few lessons have demonstrated, when students are exposed to lots of books, they are also exposed to lots of good ideas about topics, structure, styles, patterns, organization, and many other tools for expressing themselves. Using students' favorite writers as our "co-teachers" is a great way to help students grow.

SKILL FOCUS

Borrowing from our favorite authors (ideas)

RESOURCES

Books that show good ideas

QUICK HINTS

In your writing center, display a poster entitled, "I want to write like..." Invite students to add authors' names and what they like about their writing as they come across good books, beautiful lines, colorful illustrations, and clever ideas that they would like to emulate. Be sure to add those that inspire you, too!

STEPS

1. This lesson is virtually a book talk. Gather some of the books you've been reading aloud to your first graders.

2. Remind them of the unique ideas that authors have for their books and that students might want to try in their own writing. Your sharing time might sound like this:

   "Boys and girls, today I want us to think about many of the books we've been reading lately. We all have our favorite authors, and we love the books they write for us. We've found that authors are really creative. Sometimes I find myself reading a book and saying to myself, 'I wish I'd thought to write about that.' Do you ever say that to yourselves? Today I want us to think about the great ideas authors have had and how we can use some of their ideas for our own writing. We don't want to copy the words of writers, but we can borrow some of their ideas. Let me show you some books that I think show us good ideas..."

3. Some books and the good ideas we might borrow:
   Fun, No Fun by James Stevenson. This is a delightful book with different formats for listing and illustrating what the young speaker thinks is either "fun" or "no fun."
   When I Was Five by Arthur Howard. In the first half of the book, a six-year-old tells what he liked at age five; in the second half, he tells what he likes now.
   Quick as a Cricket by Audrey Wood. In this book of similes, the author compares the traits of the character to the traits of various animals—just as in the title.
   That's Good! That's Bad! by Margery Cuyler. Using the typical pattern of a story that changes back and forth from good to bad, this book takes a little boy on a wild journey.
   There's an Ant in Anthony by Bernard Most. The author has fun with word chunks as Anthony searches for more "ants" in words.

Using captions and illustrations

EXPLANATION: Capturing the main ideas and thoughts of what has been read or studied is a valuable skill. Students may find that using illustrations along with captions is an easy way to express the main ideas of what they've read or learned. Using illustrations also taps the artistic talents of many children.

SKILL FOCUS

Using captions and illustrations to show main ideas

MATERIALS

Reading selection (suggested: *Beetles* by Claire Llewellyn)

QUICK HINTS

This lesson is also a great way to teach content-area material. After reading a section of material, have students stop to illustrate and summarize with a caption what they've learned. This is great for developing keen listening skills, too!

STEPS

1. Choose a book that provides short passages which can easily be summarized in one sentence, and that lend themselves to illustrations. Nonfiction works well. *Beetles* by Claire Llewellyn is a good choice.

2. First, read a short selection (for example, pages 8 and 9 of *Beetles*—a short chapter entitled, "Where Do They Live?").

3. Talk aloud and retell what you just read: "In this chapter, the author told us that beetles live on high mountains and in low deserts. They also live in rain forests and underwater. They live in dry, hot places but also in the Arctic where it's very, very cold and icy. The only place they don't live is in salt water. Hmmm…I think the author is telling us that beetles live almost everywhere on Earth!"

4. Tell students: "I'm going to draw a picture here to show what I learned, and I'm going to label it with what I think is the main idea of this chapter."

5. Let students try this exercise with a chapter that you read to them. Explain: "With our pictures and captions we're summarizing, which means that we're using only a few words to tell what a longer story or text is all about. When you summarize, you use the fewest words possible. You don't give the details, only the most important idea that the writer is sharing."

Beetles live almost everywhere on Earth

Section Six:
Publishing Our Writing

Nothing motivates students to write and to produce better writing more than publishing! All students love the feeling of being published authors of compositions they've spent time developing. They love the feeling of having a product that classmates and others will read and enjoy. That's why teachers give students the opportunity to publish writing in many forms in the classroom. There's nothing like the pride of a child whose classmates are celebrating her as a new author as she presents her newly published book!

There are many different ways to publish student works. Publishing in the Writing Workshop has a broad definition. It means any format that allows writing to be shared with others. This can be as simple as hanging writing on a special bulletin board in the classroom or in the hallway for others to see. It can mean reading a composition aloud to classmates or displaying it on a special shelf in the reading center. Publishing can also be as sophisticated as binding the writing into a beautiful book with a cover designed by the young author.

Above: A student reads his writing from the Author's Chair.
Below: Students' writings can be published in individual books.

Early in the school year, we begin publishing informally by putting some of our best pieces of writing on the bulletin board, or we bind our individual or interactive writing together into a class book. Our class books are some of the students' very favorite books to read, especially during independent reading time. And this simple publishing process provides an audience and purpose for writing early on.

Later in the year, we may move into publishing individual books. We wait a bit to do that, until students' work is considered "worthy" of publishing. We've found that if we do formal publishing in the form of a book too early in the year, students don't learn to value some pieces of their writing above others. Students must learn to be discriminating in their writing. They need to see, just like adults, that some of their writing is fine, some is not so good, and other pieces show great potential. Those pieces that show potential are the ones to revise and publish. Students have enough pride in these pieces that they'll carefully attend to revising and editing to the extent that they're able to.

The special pieces chosen for publication get our attention, too, in individual conferences where we develop students according to what they need. We develop the whole class in our mini-lessons, but

Students' writings also can be published in class books and through displays.

we have time during conferences to nurture students individually. We appreciate these conferences, especially in classes where there is great diversity in skills. Some students might be ready to work on developing their ideas with concrete examples or varying their sentence constructions, while others need additional work on basics—writing complete sentences, spacing between words, or putting end punctuation in appropriate places. Although individual conferences and lessons are

not a focus of this book, please know that they are critical for guiding students according to their own needs.

The lessons in this section share a variety of ways to publish throughout the year, starting with class books and little books in the early part of the year, and ending with more formal bookmaking. Templates in the Appendix will help make publishing easier for you. Have a wonderful time celebrating your young authors this year!

Class books

EXPLANATION: Kindergarten children begin their publishing experience with class charts of patterned sentences and then pieces that are written by the class. This type of publishing continues and is extended in first grade. Class books offer excellent models for the many individually authored books that will follow. Classes may spend a week or more working on this focused lesson.

SKILL FOCUS

Publishing class books

QUICK HINTS

Class charts of patterned sentences can be displayed by hanging them on a coat hanger and then hanging on a coat rack. (See photo, below.)

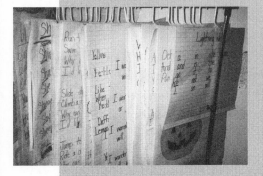

You might also display books by attaching silver rings to them and hanging them by hooks on pegboard.

STEPS

1. Choose from the many topics for class books. Explore topics that relate to a theme, such as how to play, how to cook, or how to spend a vacation. For example, brainstorm topics for a class book on How to Eat an/a…

orange	pizza	popsicle
apple	hot dog	ice cream cone

2. After choosing a topic, model writing a "how to" paragraph. For example:

   How to Eat an Orange
   Choose an orange that is firm and bright orange in color. Punch a hole in one end and peel away the skin. Divide the orange into sections. Remove the white strings and seeds. Eat one section at a time. Enjoy the juicy, sweet fruit.

3. Point out to students how the order of the steps is really important in a "how to" piece of writing.

4. Have students choose a topic from the class brainstorm list and write on "How to Eat a/an____."

5. Through individual and group conferences, help students to make their writing clean and clear for publishing.

6. Collect the individual papers and bind or staple them into a class book titled *Our "How to Eat" Stories!*

Little books

EXPLANATION: Publishing in any format really motivates students. When they know that others will read their writing, they usually take great pride in their work. The promise of publishing helps students set higher goals for their writing. The little books in this mini-lesson allow students to publish with a minimum of effort on the teacher's part and also allow students to carry home many of their publishing attempts.

SKILL FOCUS

Publishing little books

MATERIALS

11-by-14-inch unlined paper (one sheet per student) folded into books (see Appendix, page 113).

QUICK HINTS

Little books can be used for a variety of purposes. Have students use them to:
- Take notes during reading or listening.
- Record the literary elements of a story (one page each for characters, setting, problem/solution, plot, main idea/theme)
- Collect interesting words from reading
- Make a pictionary of words for guided reading.
- Publish short poems

STEPS (multiple days)

1. Early in the year, tell students that they will all get to publish a book to take home soon. Before they publish, model for them how to transfer a draft of your writing into a little book. Choose a short piece of writing that you wrote earlier, one that you liked. For example:

   My First Plane Trip

   My first plane trip was so much fun, even though I was a little scared at first. / Flying above the fluffy clouds was so beautiful! / I loved having the little table to pull down to eat on and to write on. / They gave us peanuts and drinks, too. / I loved my very first plane trip!

2. Edit your work carefully for publication.

3. Explain the parts of the little book that will make it like a real published book. Each time you explain a part of the text, stop and transfer your information to that page. The parts are:
   - The title page for your book title and name.
   - The dedication page, where you choose someone special to honor with this book.
   - The story pages—five pages to write and illustrate your writing (Show students the back slashes (/) you put in your writing where you plan to divide it into pages. Later, help them to decide where these will go in their own writing.)
   - The about-the-author page, with a bit of information about the author—you!

4. After modeling each page, you now have a little published book ready to share with others! Allow students to turn one of their writing pieces into a book. (See Appendix, page 113 for a template with directions for making a little book.)

Informational little books

EXPLANATION: Some students appreciate learning a structure that helps them to organize an informational piece of writing. This lesson shows students how the little book format can be a graphic organizer. Don't require students to follow this exact format each time they write information pieces, as many of them will be capable of extending their writing beyond this brief format.

SKILL FOCUS

Learning informational structure through little books

MATERIALS

- 11-by-14-inch unlined paper folded into little books (see Appendix, page 113, for template.)
- *From Caterpillar to Moth* by Jan Kottke

QUICK HINTS

The little book can easily become an observation journal. Set up a science center that requires students to visit now and then and to record observations in their little books. They might record in words or pictures observations on:
- The changes over time in a partially eaten apple in a jar.
- How the class pet eats, plays, and grows.
- The way mold grows on bread over time.

STEPS

1. Tell students that you want to write an informational book using some things you've learned from a book you've read in class. The book used for this lesson is *From Caterpillar to Moth* by Jan Kottke.

2. If students already know that a little book includes a page for the title, the dedication, and author information, tell them that your informational book will use the middle pages to:
   - Tell the reader what your book is about in one sentence.
   - Give the reader an interesting fact about your topic.
   - Give the reader a second interesting fact about your topic.
   - Give the reader a third interesting fact about your topic.
   - Summarize what your book was about.

3. Model each of the pages for the informational book you're writing to fit this outline. For example:

Page 1	Title: How Caterpillars Become Moths
Page 2	Dedication: To my wonderful first-grade class
Page 3	It is interesting to see how moths grow.
Page 4	Moths lay eggs on leaves.
Page 5	The eggs hatch into caterpillars.
Page 6	Soon the caterpillar spins a cocoon and lives in it for the winter.
Page 7	Then the moth comes from the cocoon, and soon it will lay eggs.
Page 8	Include information about yourself on the about-the-author page.

4. Enjoy illustrating all of the pages of your little book and then put it in the classroom for students to enjoy.

5. Encourage your students to write an informational book about something they're interested in. Furnish them with the folded little books.

Talking about writing

EXPLANATION: Just as we want students to learn to talk about books they're reading, we also want them to talk about what they're writing. Conversations about writing help students build confidence in their abilities as readers and writers. Sharing should start early in the year, so that students will get ideas from each other about topics.

SKILL FOCUS

Learning to converse about the craft of writing (sharing)

MATERIALS

- A piece of writing from an earlier lesson
- Share chair (optional)

QUICK HINTS

Make a special "share chair" for students to sit in as they share their writing. It's not expensive: just paint a hard plastic lawn chair with colorful designs using glitter paint. Consider giving students a permanent marker and letting them autograph the chair when they share or when they publish. You might even raffle off the chair at the end of the year, allowing someone to carry home a souvenir of all their classmates!

STEPS

1. Tell students that you want them to have time each day to talk about their writing so that they can learn things from each other. Explain that sometimes they'll simply share with a table buddy what they've been working on. Other times you'll want a couple of them to come and sit in a special place to share with the whole class. Present your "share chair" if you have one.

2. On a piece of chart paper or on poster board, make a list of things you can tell about your writing when you share. Get students' ideas, too. Your list might look something like this:

   When I Share My Writing

   I can tell...

   > *...how I got my idea.*
   > *...how long I worked on it.*
   > *...whether I think I need to keep working on it.*
   > *...what else I might add to it.*

   I can ask my classmates...

   > *...if there's anything they'd like to know more about.*
   > *...if they can picture what I've written.*
   > *...if they've ever written anything like my piece.*

3. Read aloud one of your written pieces. The piece on page 100 (the multiple-day writing lesson) is a good example.

4. Using the sharing chart as a guide, share a couple of items from the "I can tell..." section. Ask students for feedback, using the "I can ask my classmates..." section as a guide.

5. Tell students you'll leave the chart up in the room to help them as they talk about their work. Convince them that it's fun to talk about what they've been working on!

Publishing at last!

EXPLANATION: Once your beginning writers have written several first drafts, help them choose one to take all the way through the writing process to publishing. Model this process with this mini-lesson.

—**SKILL FOCUS**—

Choosing a piece to publish

—**MATERIALS**—

Several first drafts written by you

—**QUICK HINTS**—

If first drafts are written in a spiral notebook or sewn-in composition book, it is easier to choose from three to five that might be ready to publish since the drafts are kept together. Young writers need one-on-one help in choosing a piece to publish. Ask them to sign up for a conference when they have written three to five first drafts. Then meet with them to assist in choosing a piece to publish.

STEPS

1. Refer back to three or four first drafts that you have modeled for the class. Talk about each one, discussing what you like and don't like. You may like them all, but your task is to look for one piece of writing that's a little special.

2. Think aloud about who will be reading the published piece. Considering the audience helps us decide which piece is best for publishing. Let students know that published writing will be displayed in the hall for other students to read. Use this knowledge to choose one of your pieces. If one is about when your cat destroyed a flower arrangement, one is about your son getting lost at the state fair, and one is about a family picnic, your decision-making process might sound like this:

    "Boys and girls, you really laughed when I wrote about the cat and the flowers torn to shreds, but I need to add more details to make it a good piece to publish. The family picnic was fun for me to write about, but I didn't think you enjoyed it as much as I did. But we all enjoyed the piece about Max getting lost at the fair, and the happy ending surprised all of you. Yes, this is the one that I want to publish, so that everyone who walks by our classroom can enjoy it, too!"

3. Tell students to talk with a partner about several of their own first drafts. Let the partner help them decide which is the best choice to publish. Set a timer so that discussion time is limited.

Cleaning up our final drafts

EXPLANATION: After students select a first draft to publish, they'll need to take certain steps to ensure that the piece is cleaned up for public view. Most teachers allow students to write many more first drafts than they publish so that they focus on content and organization rather than mechanics.

SKILL FOCUS

Cleaning up our final drafts

QUICK HINTS

There is no hard and fast rule for how much of the cleaning up of final drafts should be done by the student and how much by you. Some students require more help than others. Remember that young writers are just starting out on this exciting writing journey.

It isn't always necessary for the child to do the copying of his or her final draft. Volunteers can assist by typing in the writing on a word processor.

STEPS

1. Remind students that they take the first step in cleaning up final drafts when they use the Quick Check procedures (see page 50) . If necessary, review the Quick Check list and how it's useful for catching basic mechanical errors, such as spelling, punctuation, and capitalization. This is a self-edit.

2. Instruct students as to how you want them to sign up or in some say indicate that they are ready for a publishing conference. Explain that you will use the conference time to work with them, reading over their pieces to look for ways to make them better. Share with them that you want them to be proud of their writing, and that since it will be in public view, it must be easy to read. Tell them that during the conference you will put a dot at the end of a line that contains an error and ask them to go back and find and fix the problem. Words that are spelled incorrectly must be corrected. (Most teachers assist students with spelling in the final draft so that students will continue to use interesting but hard-to-spell words.)

3. Use a previously written piece of yours to model the above steps of cleaning up a final draft. If the students see you talk through the thinking process involved, they will be more likely to do much of the cleaning up on their own.

Formats for publishing

EXPLANATION: Using a variety of publishing formats motivates students to write. Providing an audience for their writing shows them that they have something important to say.

SKILL FOCUS

Formats for publishing

QUICK HINTS

When using the book template in the Appendix (pages 114–117), consider these hints:

- Each full-page template is to be cut in half to create two pages. One complete template makes two books.
- You might want to copy and store stacks of the pages in the publishing center for students to use as they need them.
- You might want volunteers to prepare bound books for the publishing center using the template and including different lengths of middle pages: 3, 6, 9, 12. You can help students make the decision about which pre-made book is appropriate for the length of their final copy.

STEPS

1. Discuss with the class the many ways that their writing can be published. For example:
   a. Display samples of class and individual little books from the year before.
   b. Show students the empty resealable bags on a bulletin board waiting for their writing.
   c. Take them on a tour of the room and areas in the hall where work will be displayed.
   d. Point out that the writing center has special types and sizes of paper to use for publishing.
   e. Display a 3-ring binder holding clear plastic sheet protectors with each child's name on a label in the corner. This notebook will serve as an ongoing receptacle for published work.

2. Have students choose a piece to be published and the format for the display.

3. Continue to publish class books in which each student contributes a page. A construction paper cover with the title and authors' names will motivate students to publish.

4. Publish books with writing from small groups of students. Divide the class into four groups, and have each group write on a different topic.

Appendix

Flip Card Instructions

Mini-Lesson: Apostrophes in Contractions, Page: 57

Directions: (They look more complicated than they are!)

1. Fold an unlined sheet of paper (8 ½-by-11-inch) in half lengthwise.

2. Unfold the paper and then fold the edges of both long sides into the middle, using the first fold as a guideline for the midpoint.

3. Cut along the midpoint to separate the paper into two parts.

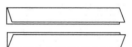

4. Cut each long folded section in half, starting at the midpoint of the folded edge, to make four equal sections.

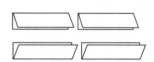

5. On each section, write the contraction you're studying, such as *he'll*, in large print on the top fold.

6. On each section, make a cut before the apostrophe to form a flap.

7. On each section, raise the top left flap and write another pronoun that can be used to form a contraction in the same way, such as *she*.

8. On each section, raise the top right flap and write the verb which is shortened by the apostrophe, such as *will*.

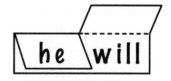

9. Invite students to have fun making different words and contractions with the Flip Cards!

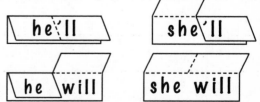

Sequence Book Instructions

Mini-Lesson: Sequencing—Part Two, Page 69

Directions:

1. Fold one sheet of unlined paper (8 1/2-by-11-inch) downward in half.

2. Bring the sides together to fold in half again and crease all folds.

3. Unfold and cut the paper from the top middle to the center of the fold lines.

 cut

4. Fold down the top left section.

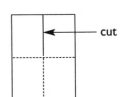

5. Fold the bottom left section to the right.

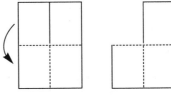

6. Fold down the top right flap.

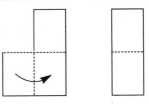

7. The top flip becomes the cover of the book.

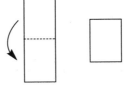

Title

8. Number the pages of the book as shown.

Inside		Outside	
4	1	Title	5
3	2		6

Little Book Instructions

Mini-Lesson: Publishing little books, Page 100
Activity: Making the little book

Directions

1. Take a piece of 8¹/₂-by-11-inch paper (or larger if you want) and fold it lengthwise (the hotdog fold). Neatness counts!

2. Fold the paper in half again from top to bottom.

3. Fold it one more time in half from top to bottom..

4. Unfold the whole paper and fold it widthwise (the hamburger fold).

5. From the middle of the folded edge, cut or tear the paper straight down the crease until you get to the intersection of the creases.

6. Unfold the paper again and fold lengthwise.

7. Hold the paper in both hands, one on each end. Slowly push your hands together until the middle tents into a diamond shape. Keep pushing the edges together until all of the edges come together.

8. Grab the pages and fold them all in one direction until they form a little book.

This is a book that won't fall apart and doesn't require staples, tape, etc. They can also be used for vocabulary books, poetry books, fact/note gathering, etc.—there are a million different uses!

_____

Title

This story was
written and illustrated by

_____

Author's name

- -

_____

Title

This story was
written and illustrated by

_____

Author's name

✳✳✳✳✳✳✳

This book is dedicated to

_____

Author's name

✳✳✳✳✳✳✳

This book is dedicated to

_____

Author's name

About the author...

_____

_____

_____

_____

_____

_____

About the author...

_____

_____

_____

_____

_____

_____

About the author…

_____ is _____ years

old. _____ is in _____

_____ class in the _____

grade. _____ likes

to _____ at

school. _____ likes to _____

at home. This is the _____ book that

_____ has written this year.

About the author…

_____ is _____ years

old. _____ is in _____

_____ class in the _____

grade. _____ likes

to _____ at

school. _____ likes to _____

at home. This is the _____ book that

_____ has written this year.

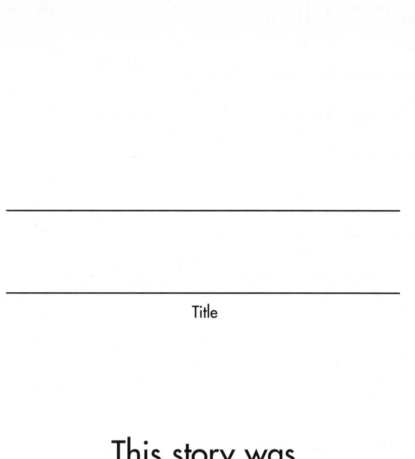

_____

_____

Title

This story was
written and illustrated by

_____

Author's name

About the Author:

_____

is _____ years old.

_____hobbies

are_____

_____.

This is the _____ book

published by _____.

The Important Poem

The important thing about... _____

_____.

_____

_____

_____

_____

_____

_____

But the most important thing about... _____

_____.

Instructions for Making Envelopes for Friendly Letters, Invitations, and Thank-You Notes

Mini-Lessons: Friendly letters; Invitations; Thank-you notes; Pages: 80–82

Materials: One sheet of 8¹/₂-by-11-inch paper (can be a sheet of notebook paper)

Smooth down all of the creases as you fold and your envelope will be much nicer!

1. Turn a sheet of paper sideways and bring the top corners down until the edges meet in the middle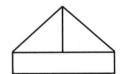

2. Bring the bottom edge up until it meets the bottom of the folded edges.

3. Fold the entire edge that's below the triangle up.

4. Overlap the bottom edges equally and press the folded edges.

5. Now tuck one of the flaps inside the other (it doesn't matter which one).

6. Seal your envelope with tape or stickers.

You might even write your letter on the paper you're making into an envelope so that you'll have a letter and envelope all in one!

Bibliography

Professional References

Calkins, Lucy M. et al. *Living Between the Lines*. Portsmouth, NH: Heinemann, 1990.

Cunningham, P. M.; Hall, D.P.; Sigmon, C. M. *The Teacher's Guide to Four-Blocks®*. Greensboro, NC: Carson-Dellosa Publishing Co., Inc, 1999.

Cunningham, P.M.; Hall, D.P.; Cunningham, J.W. *Guided Reading the Four-Blocks Way®*. Greensboro, NC: Carson-Dellosa Publishing Co., Inc., 2000.

Graves, Donald. "The Child, the Writing Process and the Role of the Professional." Petty (Ed.), *The Writing Process of Students*. Buffalo: State University of New York.

Hillocks, G., Jr. "Research on written composition: New directions for teaching." Urbana, IL: National Conference on Research in English/ERIC Clearinghouse on Reading and Communication Skills, 1986.

Hillocks, G., Jr., & Smith, M. W. "Grammars and literacy learning." In J. Flood, D. Lapp, J. R. Squire, & J. M. Jensen (Eds.), *Handbook of Research on Teaching the English Language Arts* (2nd ed.; pp. 721–737). Mahwah, NJ: Erlbaum, 2003.

Standards for the English Language Arts, 1996. NCTE and IRA, p.37

Children's Books and Resources Cited

Brown, Margaret Wise. *The Important Book*. Harper Trophy, 1990.

Bunting, Jane. *Children's Visual Dictionary*. DK Publishing, Inc., 1995.

Cuyler, Margery. *That's Good! That's Bad!* Henry Holt & Co., Inc., 2002.

Day, Alexandera. *Carl*. Farrar Straus & Giroux, 1992.

DeRolf, Shane. *The Crayon Box That Talked*. Random House, 1997

Dickens, Charles. *A Christmas Carol*. Bantam Classics, 1999.

Dr. Seuss. *How the Grinch Stole Christmas*. Random House, 2000.

Elhert, Lois. *Growing Vegetable Soup*. Voyager Books, 1990

Florian, Douglas. *in the swim*. Harcourt Brace and Company, 1997.

Fox, Mem. *Possum Magic*. Omnibus Books, 1983.

Henkes, Kevin. *Owen*. Greenwillow Books, 1993

Henkes, Kevin. *Chrysanthemum*. Greenwillow Books, 1991

Hoffman, Mary. *Amazing Grace.* Scott Foresman, 1991.

Hopkins, Lee Bennett. *Best Friends.* Harper and Row Publishers, 1986.

Howard, Arthur. *When I Was Five.* Voyager Books, 1996.

Jenkins, Martin. *Chameleons Are Cool.* Scholastic, 1997.

Lewis, J. Patrick. *Doodle Dandies: Poems That Take Shape.* Atheneum Books for Young Readers, 1998.

Lewis, J. Patrick. *A Hippopotamusn't and Other Animal Poems.* Dial Books, 1990.

Levy, Elizabeth. *The Mystery of the Missing Dog.* New York: Invisible, Inc. Scholastic Trade, 1995.

Levy, Judith S. *Scholastic First Dictionary.* Scholastic Trade, Inc., 1998.

Llewellyn, Claire. *Beetles (Minibeasts).* Franklin Watts, 2002.

Numeroff, Laura. *If You Give a Mouse a Cookie.* Harper Collins, 1994.

Numeroff, Laura. *If You Give a Moose a Muffin.* Harper Collins Publisher, 1994.

Rockwell, Anne and Halsey, Megan. *One Bean.* Walker and Co., 1998.

Rosenberg, Erin. *May I Go Out?* Modern Curriculum Press, 1995

Ryan, Pam. *One Hundred Is a Family.* Hyperion Press, 1996.

Rylant, Cynthia. *Henry and Mudge Take the Big Test.* Simon and Schuster, 1996.

Schertle, Alice. *A Lucky Thing.* Harcourt Brace and Company, 1999.

Slingsby, Janet. *Bear's Dream.* Scholastic, 1999.

Stevenson, James. *Fun, No Fun.* Greenwillow, 1994.

Swanson, Maggie. *The American Heritage Picture Dictionary.* Houghton Mifflin Company, 1998.

Viorst, Judith. *Alexander and the Terrible, Horrible, No Good, Very Bad Day.* Aladdin Books, 1987.

Warrick, Karen Clemens. *If I Had a Tail.* Rising Moon, 2001.

Wood, Audrey. *Quick as a Cricket.* Child's Play of England, 1998.